10X MINDSET HABITS

INSPIRING STORIES AND STRATEGIES THAT WILL HELP YOU 10X YOUR MINDSET

MARCOS OROZCO, JOAO RIOS, SPENCER DAVIDSON, ANGIE TABIO, ANTHONY SANTANGELO, ALEX NAVA

I0045088

10X Mindset Habits

Copyright © 2018

All rights reserved. This book may not be reproduced in any form, in whole or in part (beyond the copying permitted by U.S. Copyright Law, Section 107, "fair use" in teaching or research, Section 108, certain library copying, or in published media by reviewers in limited excerpts), without written permission from the authors.

This book is licensed for your personal enjoyment only. This book may not be resold without written permission of the publisher. Thank you for respecting the hard work of the authors.

Disclaimer:

Thank you for buying and reading this book. The information in this book can potentially improve the quality of your life and the lives of others. If you find any mistakes, PLEASE tell us by sending the error and page you found it on to our email Info@BookFamous.com We thank you and appreciate your feedback.

While best efforts have been used, the authors are not offering legal, accounting, medical or any professional advice and make no representations or warranties of any kind and assume no liabilities of any kind with respect to the accuracy or completeness of the contents and specifically disclaim any implied warranties of merchantability or fitness of use for a particular purpose, nor shall the authors be held liable or responsible to any person or entity with respect to any loss or incidental or consequential damages caused, or alleged to have been caused, directly or indirectly, by the information or programs contained herein. The views expressed are those of the authors alone, and should not be taken as expert instruction or commands. The reader is responsible for his or her own actions. Adherence to all applicable laws and regulations, including international, federal, state, and local governing professional licensing, business practices, advertising, and all other aspects of doing business in the United States or any other jurisdiction is the sole responsibility of the purchaser or reader. Neither the authors nor the publisher assumes any responsibility or liability whatsoever on the behalf of the purchaser or reader of these materials. www.BookFamous.com (888) 266-5387

Table of Contents

Introduction

One core component of personal development is helping others along on our shared path towards being our best. In this book, I join in with five other authors from the 10X Nation. We met at the first 10X Growth Conference in Hollywood, Florida in 2017. We all take imperfect action and strive to be our very best. All of us are proof positive that a 10X Mindset can work wonders in your life.

We are all at different levels on our journeys to excellence and success. We have all overcome a wide variety of challenges and are now on the path to achieving our personal greatness. We have a wealth of stories and strategies to share that will inform, guide and inspire you to develop your own powerful Mindset.

Think of this book as having a team of coaches and mentors to assist and motivate you, and as a resource you can turn to time and again on your upward trajectory of personal development toward living your dreams. By helping you become better we also better ourselves. And know that with a focused Mindset and the right strategies and habits, anything is possible.

How to maximize and 10X your use of this book:

The biggest challenges for most people including some of the authors in this book is to stay consistent in their excellence. If you want to reach greater levels and achieve more, what really matters are the positive daily habits we do and develop every day.

The back part of this book is designed as a hybrid journal/ workbook to help you become more disciplined in your daily habits.

We put together a general checklist of 6 things you can do daily that will help you develop incredible habits and a keep you consistent. Odds are you probably do some of these things already. If you don't, I invite you to try them and I promise, if you have an open mind and a positive attitude, these daily practices can potentially change your life in a major way.

We also included a section to write down your monthly goals daily. The more you write them down, the more they are engrained into your identity and mind.

My favorite thing to do every night is to write down "What went well today" I journal every victory big or small. This builds momentum with victories and reminds us that we are on the right path.

And finally, we have a "To Do" section designed to be filled out at night before you go to bed. This mentally prepares you for the next day. It also allows your thoughts to rest easy as your subconscious mind knows that you are prepared to get things done.

Keep in mind, no one is perfect. If you fail to be consistent everyday, keep trying... Don't just quit. Get back on that horse and try again and again until you get the desired result. Wishing you the very best of luck!

Chapter One

From Ghetto to Greatness

Marcos Orozco

L os Angeles was a war zone when I was growing up. Rival gangs killed each other over drug turf regularly, killing their intended targets and innocent people alike. Bullets weren't picky about who they hit. My friends and I were constantly getting shot at by gang members. By the time I graduated high school, I had attended more funerals than I can remember.

So what's a young, ambitious, misguided, stoned, baggy pants wearing teenager holding a 40 oz. bottle of malt liquor supposed to do? Yup.. You guessed it.. I decided to plan my own funeral.

The interesting thing about that is, I don't think I was the only one who didn't see a life past 20. I was only 17 years young. I remember vividly the exact moment the idea came to me while smoking a chronic joint at my friend's funeral. We called him Little Smokey. He was a good kid who got shot with a 22-caliber gun. Those tiny bullets hit your bones and travel within your body causing a lot of internal damage. He died in the hospital during the surgery. At his funeral, I noticed a smaller guest turnout than the usual burials I've attended.

I remember thinking to myself: when I die I'm going to have the biggest funeral ever. Did I mention I was ambitious? I had it all figured out. I had a location, a guest list and had even picked out a song for my guests to remember me by. I chose a convenient cemetery location for my friends to come visit me and pour a little sip for "the dead homie" as they blazed a joint in my memory. I could see them laughing as they shared stories of all the crazy things I use to do. In my black leather wallet, I even carried a list of names and phone numbers written on a white piece of paper, so that when the police found me shot dead in the street, they could hand it over to my mother. I would occasionally remind her to be sure to call every name with a phone or pager (beeper) number on that list and invite them to my funeral. I wanted to have a last hurrah celebration and wanted my friends to celebrate our short-lived friendship.

And I had a lot of friends to invite. Over the years of going to church with my mother, having my dad drive me to play baseball, and hanging out with my "hood" friends and tagging walls, I met and connected to a lot of kids. Most of these kids had good parents like mine, but like I said, the street violence and bullets don't discriminate. I was sort of a diplomat back in those days. Even though I was from a different crew, I knew a lot of people and even rivals from different cities. To be honest, I was a better networker as a youth than I am now. Somehow I survived bullets, drugs, alcohol, depression and even homelessness. Even though during those times there were dark moments, it's now obvious that God had bigger plans for me.

The things I'm about to share with you are just a sliver of my story. I just want to share some basic Mindset habits and principles that can help you create an awesome life. I wish I could tell you it's been easy for me. But the truth is it has been anything but easy. I wish I could tell you that I had the perfect family, like the ones I grew up watching on primetime television on "Family Ties," "Who's the Boss" and "The Cosby Show." But it wasn't.

My parents divorced when I was 15. Bless them both for teaching my sisters and I values. I grew up in a small city called Gardena. A great little diverse city that happened to be located in between Compton and South

Central, which were both famous for gang violence and drug wars. If you grew up in my hood, you had to be affiliated to a local gang or graffiti crew. Our role models were local drug dealers, gang bangers and rappers.

Keep in mind, this is Los Angeles during the great crack epidemic and when gangsta rap was blaring over the radio airways. N.W.A. Eazy-E, Ice-T, DJ Quik, and Snoop Dog were local rappers who had become idols to us. We would often run into other famous rappers at the Compton Indoor Swap Meet, local malls or at the club. These were the times when 2Pac roamed the streets of L.A. My girlfriend was a waitress back then and was lucky enough to meet Biggie Smalls and Tupac Shakur when they were still good friends. They gave her both of their autographs on the same napkin. Talk about quick eBay money.

I want to share with you how my Mindset went from being hopeless and homeless to becoming a father, author and entrepreneur. With that being said, I still truly feel I have just scratched the surface of my potential. But without a shadow of a doubt, I can tell you this, it all began and changed with a positive Mindset.

I wasn't born in "the hood." I was born in Matagalpa, Nicaragua. My father, mother, my older sister and myself fled the post-revolutionary regime. We were lucky enough to come to the United States with green cards. We lived in Redondo Beach, CA for a little while – a picture postcard community on the Pacific Ocean. Life was good. Then for some unknown reason, my father decided to move us to Gardena. We're talking about a different environment like night and day.

Coming from a revolutionary war in Central America, we didn't know there was a different kind of war in the streets of Los Angeles. As soon as we moved to Gardena, I noticed differences in the culture. The streets marked with graffiti, the kids were a little rougher, and I had no choice but to adapt to my environment. The rappers and gang bangers I would come to idolize, like all the kids around me, became my role models. We glorified that deadly lifestyle and accepted that death was part of that game we played.

As far as I'm concerned, I am now living on bonus time. I shouldn't be alive. I've been shot at countless times. I've been close to getting hit by cars, I jumped off of tall places for a chance at fame and glory as I wrote my name on walls, like some of the rest of the misguided youth around me.

Only after another good friend of mine named Brian was murdered, I finally decided it was time to disconnect from the streets. That was one death more than I wanted to accept because he was such a nice guy. I wanted to become a "regular person," somebody who had a job instead of selling weed and LSD to friends and partygoers at underground raves.

That's when I decided to put on a nice shirt and pants and go look for work selling cars. I was going to beat the odds. I wanted to become somebody. I wanted to make my mother and father proud.

I didn't know what I was doing when I was hired. As a matter of fact, when I looked in the mirror I just saw a hoodlum that happened to have a job. I knew that how I saw myself was crucial if I was going to make this transition. This is when I started working on my identity. I changed my mindset from a hoodlum who had a job, to an aspiring businessman. That is no small shift, but it was life-changing. That's when things started to pick up for me. I started seeing potential and opportunities. Even my self talk started to improve.

During my time on the front lines at a Dodge dealer that had the second to worst customer service rating in the entire nation, I noticed somebody had a black TDK cassette with a small white sticker on it. Thinking it was music, I asked the guy, "What is that?"

He said, "Oh, it's just some stupid training."

"What kind of training?" I asked.

"It's for car salesman."

"Can I borrow it?"

He said, "Yeah, you can have it."

So he gave it to me. On that sticker, written in blue ink, was the name, "Grant Cardone."

I was excited about this cassette for some reason. It was almost like unwrapping a gift. On the way home from a 12-hour shift, I put it in the cassette player in my Cadillac, and played it. It was like somebody turned on a switch. I'd never heard sales training before in my life. To me, it was almost like audio pornography. It was talking about sales techniques to help you increase your closing ratios. What's interesting is that these techniques were simple, transparent and effective. I remember focusing on three simple techniques that did allow me to double my income. That's when I was hooked with self development. This was the beginning of my informal business education.

That cassette wasn't enough though. I didn't know how to find Grant Cardone, so I started looking for more training. I found lessons and dove in. This was not like anything I had learned growing up.

The first and main lesson I picked up was; "You are who you think you are." You become your identity on a conscious and subconscious level. My income didn't and couldn't change until I decided that I was a businessman and not just a hoodlum that happened to have a job at a car dealership. It was a monumental shift. My demeanor changed. My mindset changed. My daily habits improved. Some of it consciously, some of it subconsciously. I started walking with a little more pep in my step, and my confidence level was at an all-time high. I liked the person in the mirror for the first time in a long time.

Little did I know that that the decision to see myself as a businessman would alter not only my life, but the life of my son and my family. I started becoming not just a salesman but a great salesman, making a lot of money selling units at a BMW store I was now working at. But then I made a big mistake. I got caught drinking and driving on my birthday, and I was arrested. The officer also found a baggie of cocaine in my pocket. It was more like a baggie with a tiny amount of residue. I was buzzed and didn't realize it was in my pocket at the time. I ended up in jail and got slapped with a felony. During that time a friend of mine had opened an independent dealership. After a weeks of being incarcerated he came to visit me in jail. He bailed me out, but he did so under the condition that I help him open and run his new business.

That was a no brainer for me since I was probably about to get fired from the job I had anyway. I took the position of a general manager and helped him get his dealership up and running and generate revenue for the store. I soon realized he was doing unethical things that I didn't want to be part of. The money was incredible, but I decided to leave. I didn't want to tarnish my name. In the streets, a tarnished name can be bad for your health, if you know what I mean. What disturbed me is that this guy was really smart. He didn't need to resort to the shady tactics he was using. That's when I decided, "Wait, if I opened his dealership and helped him make it a success, why can't I open my own dealership?"

That leads me to the second important lesson I learned: Identify what you want out of life.

Moving on that plan to start my own business, I made a deal with a partner who was supposed to fund me with inventory for the dealership in exchange for half the profits. At the last minute, he changed his mind and pulled out of the deal. Whatever his excuse was, I now had a chip on my shoulder, and a big problem. I had already given the dealership property owner my last cent and signed the lease.

But you know what? That was the best thing that could have happened to me, because I was now committed to go all in. I didn't have any inventory, I didn't have office furniture. I had absolutely nothing but a signed lease for $7500 a month. Talk about commit first and figure it out later.

During this time, I hustled daily for about a year, often sleeping at the office. I also rented a small bedroom at my buddy's house to be near the business. I was eating on a $2 a day budget. Needless to say, the dollar menu was a blessing.

I was skinny and hungry, both physically and emotionally. But I was determined to make this happen. I was determined to succeed, because I had nothing else. I had nothing to lose. Finally I got a line of credit through the auction and I was able to buy my own cars. We were selling units, barely breaking even and sometimes losing out on deals, but I was able to keep the lights on and the doors open.

To be honest though, I was on a sinking ship. I was two months away from closing my doors, failing at my first business venture. Then, I remembered that cassette with Grant Cardone's name on it.

This was 2005. So I Googled Grant, and I realized he was coincidentally in Los Angeles. I ordered one of his CDs called "85 Automotive Closes" and used it for myself and my sales team. A week later I picked up the phone and called his office. At that time he was selling an info product on how to sell and close for employees and management for $7,500. I thought to myself, "I don't have that type of money," so I hung up and I called one of my friends who was one of my past mentors, and asked him if he wanted to go halves on this product for $7,500 and he said that I was stupid.

He said, "Why don't you just buy a car for $7,500, sell it for $9,500, and make $2,,000?" I thought to myself, "That's what I've been trying to do."

I had no cash reserves. I couldn't survive another month if I did nothing about the problem. So I made the decision and was committed to get help. Even though I didn't have the money, I picked up the phone.

Lesson number three: You have to commit.

Actually, commitment might be the first step you should take. I picked up the phone, and made the phone call. I knew I wanted this product, but I couldn't afford it, or I didn't think I could afford it. After my question and objections, the salesman passes the phone over to Grant and within a couple of minutes he identified my biggest issue and solved that problem. I didn't think I could afford it.

He said, "Look, put it on the credit card and split the payments."

I said, "Let's do it." I didn't know my credit card was going to go through, but thank God it did. I was excited about that. Four days later, a package of DVD's and workbooks came to the office. I opened it with excitement, I got the group together, everybody from the receptionist to the salesmen to the porters to my finance guy.

I committed to the vision and this sales training was now our gospel. We all bought into the ideology that this was the only solution that could get us out of the hole, and we started listening to this information on a daily basis, three times a day. And we were role playing. We were taking action. The results were incredible. We were like little Grant Cardone clones. Almost immediately we went pretty much from zero to crushing it in about a month-and-a-half to two months. The results were absolutely nothing less than a miracle.

This was the first time that I ever invested $7,500 on myself.

Lesson number four is: Invest in yourself.

One of the biggest gifts that Grant gave me was to charge me full price for the training product. It had to work for us. There was no other option. Looking back, if he would have given it to me for free, I would have been excited about it for the first couple of weeks. But odds are great that we would not have been serious about it. It might not have worked. If we didn't have any skin in the game, we would not have fully appreciated the product. A lot of entrepreneurs make the mistake of giving their expertise away to their clients. There is a saying, "If they don't pay, they don't attention." The more they pay, the more results they get, because that's just human nature. So, one of the biggest gifts that Grant gave me was to charge me full price, and as a result I had to make it work. I had no choice. I was committed.

To this day this was one of the best investments I have ever made. I remember when Grant used to have local live training. I used to close my office doors and bring everybody to the training. I used to pay for it, and my dealership was literally closed. I would leave a note in the front saying, "If you have any questions about the inventory call my number." People thought I was dumb or crazy or both for closing for a day, but when we came back to work, those were our biggest months ever. We were making deals non-stop and we were a small, independent dealership. Our average gross was $5,200, twice the national average. This is thanks to the training that Grant gave us.

Mind shift is key. It starts with that seed. It changed my life in ways I never expected.

I finally had a legit sales squad. My crew were just some regular guys who were hungry, that decided to believe in me, themselves and Grant. I have very fond memories of those times.

I grew up very humble. We always had food on our table and a roof over our head but not much else. One of my biggest mistakes during those times is that I was making so much money, I didn't have the right mentors to show me how to keep that money and how to reinvest it. During that time, I was traveling, buying boats, motorcycles, cars, clothes, you guessed it. Don't get me wrong, I enjoyed that time, but looking back, I wish I had somebody that saw my potential and taught me how to invest my money. I learned that the hard way. It was one of the many success cycles in my business career.

One of the things that you're going to learn when you get a mentor is that if you don't get the right mentor, you're going to outgrow them. And sometimes, even if you get the right mentor for that time, you will still outgrow them. They will become not just your mentors, they will now become acquaintances and equals, and you have to find mentors to get you to that next level.

One of the most difficult challenges that gets you off your game is getting comfortable.. You need 10X goals to keep you excited and hungry! With my first business, I hit a home run with a lot of hard work countless hours of working. Then I started passively investing into other businesses that didn't go well and before you know it, the great recession kicked in, and I decided to close the doors.

I got lazy, I got complacent, I got comfortable. And this is one of the most dangerous places to be as an entrepreneur. That's why it's so important to have 10X mindset, because the sad thing is that you will reach your goals if you don't think big enough. And then, you're going to think to yourself, man, I should've thought bigger.

A great book to read on this is called "The Magic of Thinking Big." Your thoughts become real things. Your emotions become real things. How you think is absolutely monumental to how you act.

Lesson number five: Choose your own environment.

I'm not talking about zip code, even though that is also a choice. Choose wisely what you absorb mentally. What are you listening to on the radio, what are you reading, what are you watching on TV if you watch TV. This is super important, as this goes into your subconscious mind, and either it empowers you or takes away from your ultimate purpose.

Get rid of all the negative people in your life. I know it's easy to say, but it's important, because they will make you doubt every step of the way, everything you do. Replace those people with like-minded people. You gotta find your crew. You have to find your tribe. If you can't find them, then create it. There's nothing more beautiful than having a group of people that have a common goal and purpose, to support you, to nurture you, and to help you get to that next level. Kind of like the authors in this group.

When I was making a ton of money, I was hanging around with bad people, just like when I was young. These were business owners, but they wanted to go to the clubs, drink, sniff coke and hook up with women, even though some of these guys were married. And I never really liked that, because of my mother and my sisters, I wouldn't like somebody doing that to them. So find your ideal tribe. If they're not out there, connect with some 10Xers, connect with the 10X Nation. This is a unique group of people that are doing things. Not saying that they're perfect, because there's some wacky ones, but most of them are solid individuals.

None of what you read really matters if you don't take consistent action. Action is monumental to everything I just said, because just reading books and consuming content, nothing happens if you don't take that first step. Pick up the phone, make that first call, take that first step towards your marathon. Do that first sit-up, empty that refrigerator, write that first word of your book. And that's where every journey eventually begins, with that first step of action. Most people overthink it.. Don't lean back. Go all in!

I just want to thank you for taking the time to read my chapter in this book. And I just want you to know as long as you don't quit, you keep taking action, and you know where you want to go, you can get there eventually. It might not be easy, it might not be fun, but I'll tell you one thing, it's so worth it. Whether we've met each other or we haven't, I want you to know that I'm rooting for you, and you're not alone. The 10X Nation is here to support!

Marcos Orozco is a speaker, multiple best selling author and founder of Book Famous. He is dedicated to helping people just like you become published authors so that they can Increase their Influence, leverage their message and expand their brand so that you can prospect like a boss and generate more revenue. In his spare time he enjoys skateboarding with his eight-year-old son and being a dad.

Chapter Two

How to Create a 10X Mindset

Angie Tabio

As far as I can remember as a little girl of four years old, I had to create a powerful Mindset. The innocence of a child is so beautiful, but when it's taken away by harmful, sick people, your whole outlook of life changes to make you either a victim or a victorious person.

I remember at the age of four years old being a sex object for the disgusting filthy old men who used to have me sit on their laps for pleasure. I remember feeling very uncomfortable and unhappy because I couldn't tell my parents. I was depressed inside, but always smiling on the outside. I became good at it because it was the only way it kept me alive.

While growing up in elementary and junior high school, I would notice other victims like me because of their body language and not wanting to associate themselves with other kids. I would approach them and ask them, "Why aren't you playing with others? Are you being molested or raped by someone, because I was." Their expression said it all, and they asked, how did I know? Once I would share with them that I was a child that was being molested by a family member, they became my friend and we supported each other. One thing that I would share with them is how I got rid of those bad feelings and emotions of wanting to kill myself. I could get rid of those thoughts by thinking about happy moments with my family and my pet animals. As an adult now, while coaching a client about her childhood experience, I can still feel at times that unhappy little girl who still comes out at times to say hello.

As I got older, by the age of 14 years old I became homeless. In my up-coming book, I will share more about that. I did not have a choice to stay as a young 14-year-old teenager because I had to learn how to survive. I learned how to spend time with my desires in life and develop more at-tention to them. At the age of 16 years old, I used to do my homework at a public library or at Barnes & Noble bookstore.

One day I was just looking at Barnes & Noble bookshelves. I was looking at the shelves around me and would read the types of books on each shelf like science, math, social studies and so on. But I then saw a shelf that read Personal Development. I was intrigued to learn what that shelf was all about, so I picked up a book that completely changed my life to become the woman I am today. The name of the book was "Think and Grow Rich" by Napoleon Hill.

That was how I was introduced to personal development and fell in love with it. I never stopped reading about personal growth, and started reading other gurus in the industry of personal development like Zig Ziglar, Jim Rohn, Dr. Wayne Dyer and Tony Robbins, to name a few. And of course my first mentor, the legendary motivational speaker Mr. Les Brown. Once you understand the power of having a powerful positive Mindset, you will realize that your goals and desires are components in a process, and that your success will come along with each step of the process. This is how I started to create a deeper powerful mindset.

To create a powerful Mindset, you need to have a goal, a vision and a desire. You must develop a plan of action. My plan of action was to make sure that I graduated from junior high school and high school without the guidance of my parents or an adult. I was a target for prostitution, to sell drugs and become part of a female gang. One thing that I thank my parents for was planting the seed of spiritual belief within the Catholic religion and building a relationship with God at a very young age.

Most of the time our mind worries, has doubts; we may have confusion, we go through depression, we may get angry and have feelings of condemnation – all these are attacks on our mind. I remember going through all these feelings that didn't feed into my purpose. If any of these are a constant companion in your life, there's a battle of an unhealthy life going on in your mind, body and soul. The good news is that you can win the battle in your mind. Thoughts are powerful, and you can overcome anything just by having the right Mindset. Believe me that in the long run, the simple questions you ask yourself on a regular basis will determine the type of person you become.

Negativity often breeds not from the answers we receive from this world, but from the questions we ask ourselves every day. If you ask yourself negative questions, you will get negative answers. There are no positive answers to:

- "Why me?"

- "Why didn't I?"

- "What if I'm not good enough?"

As a child of God, I didn't ask myself those questions because I knew in my heart that everything that I was going through in my life was because God had a plan for me. I was already making a difference at a very young age by saving lives of many children my age who wanted to commit suicide. I knew that I had a calling in my life, so I had to listen to my heart and follow my purpose and calling in life.

Think about it. Would you allow someone else to ask you the demoralizing questions you sometimes ask yourself? I doubt it. So stop and change

Ask questions that push you in a positive direction of positive mindset, because that's what I practiced. I created a culture of positive thinking for my mind, body and soul.

Here are some ideas & questions that I would ask myself to change my mindset daily:

What could you be grateful for and positive about right now, if you really wanted to? Your greatest weapon against stress and negativity is your ability to choose one thought over another every single day in a journal. Happiness escapes from those who refuse to see the good in what they have. When life gives you every reason to be negative, think positive because everything in life happens for a reason or a season. That's the positive thinking I had to practice every day growing up. Think about it: what's one problem you're thankful you don't have? Yes, smile right now, not because life has been easy, perfect or exactly as you had anticipated, but because you choose to be happy and grateful for all the good things you do have, and all the problems you know you don't have. The first thing that I do every morning is thank God that I am alive and healthy, happy and grateful for all the things that I do have and I don't have.

What are you holding on to that you need to let go of? Oftentimes holding on makes us weaker, and letting go builds our strength. Does that thing you were extremely upset about a year ago or the last two years really matter now? I bet it doesn't, and if you are still thinking about, it's not serving your best interests. That was a difficult one for me because I couldn't understand why my parents weren't there for me when I needed them the most, growing up, at the age of 14 years old. But as I got older I could understand that my parents did the best that they could with the little that they had as children, growing up themselves. I will forever be grateful to my parents for trying to be the best parents that they could be for my two sisters and brother.

Who or what needs your forgiveness? Forgiveness doesn't always lead to healed relationships and situations. Some relationships and situations aren't meant to be. Forgive anyway, and let what's meant to be, *be.* Go ahead and set yourself *free*. Remember, that this is about you, not about them. When you hold resentment toward another, you are bound to that person or condition by an emotional link that is stronger that steel. Forgiveness is the only way to dissolve that link and break free. I had to forgive my stepfather who molested my daughter at the age of four years old. I can say that it was the hardest thing for me to do because I wanted to kill him and I had it all planned. My daughter and I had to go to counseling for a year and a half. Believe me, it's a far less stressful life when you forgive and move forward in your life, even when life just does not seem fair to you. Forgiveness is what set me free, for my own well-being, because at the end its about me moving forward in my life, not any one else's.

What's something nice you can do for someone else right now? You need to do all the good you can to as many people as you can as often as you can. No act of love and kindness, no matter how small, is ever wasted. I have made it a mission in my life every day to compliment a woman who passes by me. I will compliment her about her hair, her eyes, her smile or her outfit. I never know what that woman is going through, but the moment I give her a compliment she puts on a beautiful smile of gratitude. It also makes me feel good inside and know that I have made a difference in someone's life even through it's a compliment that does not cost a thing. What compliments have you received lately?

Remember, butterflies don't know the color of their wings, but the human eyes know how beautiful they are. Likewise, in your busy days, you likely don't notice just how great you are, but others nearby still see that you are incredible and beautiful. When someone says something nice about you, it's worth remembering because good vibes always come back around to reward you.

What do you know that you're great at? Although it's nice to hear people compliment you, it's not essential to your self-worth. And if no one offers to give you a compliment, give yourself one. You start by looking yourself at the mirror and telling yourself: you are *good* enough, *smart* enough and *strong* enough. You don't need other people to validate who you are because you are *valuable*! Notice your strengths, focus on them, and celebrate them every single day of your life. I love to volunteer and offer my services to the community and non-profit organizations. I love being a servant leader to the community by leading with others in mind and by cultivating a culture of empowerment worldwide. You can too!

What would you do differently if you knew nobody would judge you? Let's face it, you can't please everyone and you shouldn't try, because we all know, unfortunately, that you can't please everyone. Let me also tell you, like my mentor Les Brown says, "What people say about you is none of your business." You need to care less about what people say about you and smile more about what you know is *true*. Live your life and be happy with yourself without their negative judgements. Practice listening to compliments and constructive criticism, and ignoring insults and negativity. It's far from easy, I know, but it's worth working on it.

I was bullied and picked on in my teenage years. There were these two girls who lived on my block and went to the same middle school as I did. These two girls were so jealous of me because of the good girl that I was and how well I was doing in school by making the dean's list. They had told everyone around my block that they were going to fight me on a specific day. I was walking from school one day and I was caught off guard and beaten up in front of all my friends. I acted brave, I walked away, and ignored what had just happened to me. The bullying continued until I said enough is enough. I told everyone from the block that this time, I will be fighting both girls. Of course, everyone was there to see how I was going to fight not one of the girls, but both. My friends from the block shared the story with everyone from school about how I confronted the girls and won the fight. I was never bullied again. Always remember that people will go as far as you allow them to!

What excuses do you need to stop making? I graduated from George Washington High School in New York. There was a quote from George Washington on the school hallway that read, "It is better to offer no excuse than a bad one." Nothing could be closer to the truth. If you are good at making excuses you will never be good at anything else. You won't always get where you intended to go in life, but you will eventually arrive precisely where you need to be. No matter what the obstacles are that you see in front of you right now, the only thing truly standing between you and what you want is the excuse you keep telling yourself as to why you can't achieve it. There is a quote from William Arthur Ward that reads, "If you can imagine it, you can achieve it. If you can dream it, you can become it."

Why am I afraid to fail? If only people knew that to grow you need to learn from your failures. If you learn from your failures, why are you always so afraid to fail? If you want to do it right, make lots of mistakes and accept a great deal of discomfort along the way. It might sound crazy, but it's worth your while. In life, failures make you smarter and discomfort makes you stronger. Both are necessary growing pains. My advice is to always embrace your failures because eventually you will arrive precisely where you need to be.

What do you now know better for next time? Don't let your fear of past events affect the outcome of your future. Live for what today must offer, not what yesterday has taken away. There will always be obstacles, but we are confined most often by the walls we build ourselves. What we see depends on how we look at it. Forget what you've lost and focus on what you've learned. Step forward, but don't rush. I want you to always remember that fear and *faith* cannot go together.

Where do I want to go next? Don't completely waste the season of life you are in now simply because you want the next one to begin. There is always beauty waiting to be realized. Notice the goodness happening around you right now, even if you must look a little harder than usual. Every unwelcome event, person or situation is just a doorway into the next you and a stronger, wiser *you*.

I want you to figure out what motivates you to grow into your most authentic self, and remember that you can't grow unless you're willing to change. Change first starts with *you*. As you grow, you'll notice you don't change much, you just become more of who you are meant to be. I want you to think, what gets you excited about life? Think about it!! If you truly wanted to be excited right now, what could you get excited about? Find it and focus on it more often. When you truly believe in what you're doing, it shows and it pays. I want you to create a visionary board. You ask, "What is a visionary board?" A vision board is a collage of images, pictures, and affirmations of your dreams, goals and things that you want to see manifest themselves. If you think vision boards are bogus, then the joke is on you. They work and there's a simple explanation of why they work so well.

Get information and examples from the author Jack Canfield (of the "Chicken Soup for the Soul" series fame) on his 21 ways to make your vision board more powerful. The best way to achieve your goals is to keep them on top of mind, so you're always looking for ways to move yourself closer to them.

I know and believe that a vision board is the perfect tool to help you do that. Success in life is for those who are excited about where they're going and doing for themselves. I want you to practice the skill of visualization. It's a skill, which means that everyone can learn it and improve it through practice. It is the ability to imagine things. This skill involves creativity and imagination. The greater the details of the mental images you create, the greater the skill. Believe me, that's how I created mine.

Two of my visualizations that I had on my visionary board and in my journal was, one, to meet Oprah Winfrey. I can say that I was blessed to have met her three years ago.If you go to my Facebook page under Angie Tabio, you will see the picture that was taken of the both of us. Also, two, I wanted to work side by side with my mentor Les Brown. Today, I am one of the faculty members of The Les Brown Institute. How cool is that! If that isn't a *dream* come true, then I don't know what is. One important thing that I must add is that you need to attach emotions to your visualization. Dreams do come *true*, but you must first visualize it and connect it with emotions.

Life is filled with unanswered questions, but it is the courage to ask enough of the right ones that ultimately leads you to an understanding of yourself and your purpose.

You can spend your life wallowing in fear by avoiding the obvious, or asking negative questions like, "Why me?" Or you can be grateful that you've made it this far and that you are strong enough to breathe, walk and think for yourself.

I want to go into details of the philosophy of personal development and how people create and live by the principles. All in all, the philosophy of personal development is about making the core principles of personal development into a philosophy of life. The philosophy of personal development is ultimately about embodying this spirit of continual progress in one's character so the bearer is now armed with the tools to boldly and consciously participate in his or her own self-actualization.

What is the philosophy of personal development?

Well, let's start from the basics; the first part of the phrase, the word philosophy is a system or way of thinking that guides our behavior. We can call this system our life philosophy. Our life philosophy consists of core principles and beliefs that dictate your actions. We use these beliefs to justify our actions or Inactions. Our beliefs tell us when to start or stop, eat and to sleep. Our beliefs tell us what is possible for your life and what is not. The philosophy of personal development is a philosophy of striving. A person may display this of striving in many forms such as in:

- Personal development

- Spiritual development/refinement

- Professional excellence

- Entrepreneurism

- Self-mastery

This may be overcoming or learning difficulties, overcoming challenges. These challenges may be the challenge thrown up in day to day life, in relationships, work, finding time to study while working two jobs, running a business, personal organization, finding motivation, physical handicaps, making your life work with a health issue or illness or learning disabilities, or working to understand and overcoming addictions.

Philosophy of life and philosophy self-actualization is as old as time. I remember my mentor Les Brown saying one day, 'Things are either growing or withering, nothing stays the same. So you have two choices: to grow and address challenges, or wither." Isn't that the truth!!! Every person in life is faced with a challenge; this is called the game of life.

So, you ask yourself, "How can the philosophy of personal development help me?" A philosophy of personal development can help you in many ways but here are my top three:

- Become your own cheerleader, cultivating a forward-moving progressive attitude. Developing your ability to motivate yourself and be more receptive to the spirit of inspiration.

- Cultivating a solution-orientated attitude.

- Cultivating a positive mental attitude though conditioning the mind with beneficial ideas. A diet of successful concepts and ideas enriches the subconscious mind positively for actions which can be applied to daily living.

In our modern era we are constantly faced with this force of change. The world of a child changes rapidly on his or her journey to adulthood. The days are gone when childhood was the only stage with rapidly expanding growth, awareness and consciousness. In order to remain relevant in the 21st Century, your knowledge, attitude and life philosophy requires continual enlightenment, in the same manner as a child experiences enlightenment.

A core principle of the philosophy of personal development is the ability to ride the waves of time, this requires:

- Flexibility: "Prepare yourself for the world, as the athletes used to do for their exercise; oil your mind and your manners, to give them the necessary suppleness and flexibility; strength alone will not do." – The words of the late Lord Chesterfield.

- Adaptability: "A wise man adapts himself to circumstances as water shapes itself to the vessel that contains it," – An unknown author.

- Being dynamic: "The pure impulse of dynamic creation is formless; and being formless, the creation it gives rise to can assume any and every form." I wish that I could take credit for this, but it's from an unknown author.

Core Principle One: Curiousness

"The searching-out and thorough investigation of truth ought to be the primary study of man." – Roman politician Marcus Cicero

Let's go back to basics: children have an innate quality that allows them to be curious, flexible, adaptable, playful and dynamic. Two of the qualities that stand out in children is curiousness and playfulness. Curiousness and playfulness are qualities shared with geniuses and pioneers; in fact, children's curiosity and playful nature is shared with all great creative people to some degree. Marcus Cicero ought to have said the searching out through thought investigation is the primary study of man and woman, because we owe our very existence on the planet to this innate drive to investigate. This curiousness or innate drive to investigate has spread the seed of humanity across the entire surface of the globe, across rivers and over mountains.

This observation of man's nature reveals man's first pillar of philosophy of personal development: inquisitiveness. Inquisitiveness is our key to freedom, which uncovers doors to new opportunity. Humanity owes its greatness to our inquisitive nature. It is this very inquisitiveness that drives the engines of personal development and growth in the infant years and all through childhood to adulthood. The results of your inquisitiveness can have great benefits in propelling you to new personal plateaus of understanding. This heightened or expanded awareness can be used to better not only your personal conditions but society as well.

Core Principle Two: Playfulness

"The master of the art of living makes little distinction between his work and his play, his labor and his leisure, his mind and his body, his education and his recreation, his love and his religion. He hardly knows which is which; he simply pursues his vision of excellence in whatever he does, leaving others to decide whether he is working or playing. To him he is always doing both." – The Buddha

Core Principle Three: Remember Your Center

"The only journey is the journey within." – Poet and novelist Rainer Maria Rilke

Rainer Maria Rilke states the simplest of all life's truths in that the only journey is the journey within. There can be no lasting value any of life's pursuits if there is no movement in your being. Every pursuit in your life's journey should cause a beneficial or valuable reorientation within. All life's pursuits are an effort to cause an inner reorientation of consciousness and awareness; this is what we call personal enlightenment. The goal of our journey is how you find value and fulfillment in the events within life's journey. On a spiritual note, everything we do in life is to add our spiritual growth. Life experience furthers the maturity or consciousness and awareness.

The philosophy of personal development is a philosophy of excellence. The quote that follows below is from the Greek philosopher Aristotle. His words are as relevant now as they were when he wrote them, and what is especially interesting is that these words could just as easily come out of the mouth of one of the modern day personal development speakers and mentors known around the world, Mr. Tony Robbins.

"Excellence is an art won by training and habituation (habit). We do not act rightly because we have virtue or excellence, but we rather have those because we have acted rightly. We are what we repeatedly do. Excellence, then, is not an act but a habit. People who apply the wisdom of a progressive philosophy, will be Invigorated and enlivened with the spirit of personal growth and power, which is found in the champions of our modern era and men and woman of old. Our beliefs make up the body of our philosophy of life and the characteristic spirit of a culture, era or community as manifested in its beliefs and aspirations."

"*Life* is as beautiful as you create it in your imagination."

Research is beginning to reveal that having a positive mindset is about much more than just being happy or displaying an upbeat attitude. A positive mindset can create real value in your life and help you build skills that last much longer than a smile. We all know the things that we can do to spark the feeling of joy, contentment and love. Only you know what things work well for you. In other words, when you are experiencing positive emotions like joy, contentment and love, you will see more possibilities in your life. There is practically no *limit* to something such as a price that can be charged or the opportunities afforded to *you*. I am the woman I am today because of my spiritual belief and my personal growth that I practice daily. *"If I can, you can too!"*

Angie Tabio is a Women's Empowerment Coach and a faculty member at The Les Brown Maximum Achievement Team. She is an inspiring leader and in-demand speaker, trainer, mentor and coach. Angie has worked with numerous leaders, entrepreneurs, organizations and nonprofit organizations for over 25 years.

Angie was one of the personal representatives for the State of Florida for over two decades raising funds for nonprofit organizations like the United Way of Miami Dade, to name one of many. She is the Vice President of the Miami Brickell Chamber of Commerce and former Director of Public Relations with the Sweetwater Chamber of Commerce.

Angie is a servant leader of her community for over 25 years, leading with others in mind by cultivating a culture of empowerment worldwide. She believes that getting things done and having a fulfilled life does not have to be self-exclusive and she can provide the necessary strategies.

Chapter Three

Is it Luck, Skill or Mindset?

Anthony Santangelo

Every success story that you read about or watch on television starts with the person being given an opportunity that they chose to capitalize on. The public will view this like that person hit the genetic lottery, or they fell into the right situation and were lucky. What they don't see is that luck has nothing to do with the person's success in the long term. I am here to show you that if I can achieve success in life, so can you! Here is my story.

I grew up in your typical middle class home a half-hour west of Philadelphia, PA, the oldest of three children, and the only boy. I went through school focusing on always trying to do the right thing, but my grades were average, which was what I like to call "the best of the worst."

My father, Tony, always told me, "Sonny, if you are going to do a job, do it right, or don't do it at all." To this day he still tells me this and still calls me Sonny! I played sports with this philosophy, whether if it was street hockey, football, basketball or my first love of baseball – always giving it my all to win the game.

My mom, Donna, a devout Christian, always made sure that I was staying in line. When I wasn't, the lectures came out, usually while we were in the car, with her making sure I knew what I did was wrong. She always ended the tongue lashing with, "Anthony, I love you, and God has a plan for you." The only plans I saw that God had for me at that time was learning how not to make excuses when I was getting in trouble. Little did I know how those "lectures" were going to play a huge part in my life.

In 1984, when I was seven years old, my Mom was diagnosed with breast cancer. Technology was not as advanced back then as it is today, and she was given two to three years to live. My parents obviously didn't tell me or my two younger sisters this, as they had other plans that superseded the doctors' plans. She beat the cancer, defying the odds until it came back four years later.

At this point, at age 11, I knew something was wrong. All I wanted was to have some peace for my family and for my Mom to get better following her surgery. Donna – God's golden soldier, as my Dad would always call her – again shocked the doctors and overcame the cancer. Four years later in 1992, the cancer reoccurred and spread to her leg. The next two years were a battle and hardship that I wouldn't wish on my worst enemy.

On August 4, 1994, my Mom, at 40 years old, finally lost her battle with cancer. I was 17, and this was a month before my senior year of high school. My sister Lori was 13 and my sister Joann was a few weeks away from turning 11. Most people would look at this tough situation and say how horrible this tragedy was. My Dad obviously took it very hard and went somewhat off the deep end. Lori felt the need to start running the household: cooking, cleaning, laundry, etc. Joann buried her head in books and used them as a distraction from the pain she felt.

As for me, the way I handled things was a little different. I had a bit of a revelation almost exactly a month prior to her passing in a tent outside Bryce National Park in Utah. I was on a Grand Canyon hiking trip with about 20 teenagers and four adults. I remember sitting in this tent by myself and coming to the realistic conclusion that if/when my Mom dies, things will be OK. This moment gave me a peace and understanding that I really can't explain other than saying it was God's grace.

When I returned home, I immediately stopped feeling the suicidal thoughts that went through my head on a weekly basis as a sophomore and junior in high school. I stopped having this hatred and anger inside of me that I only let out when I played football and hit the opposing player so hard that their ancestors felt it. Yes, I still hit hard, but I didn't have the feeling that with every tackle I was trying to push my problems on my opposition.

I think it also helped that my childhood friend, Jamison ("Jamo") Glennon, was the one who told me that my Mom had died. He and I have known each other since we were five, and are only three days apart in age. To this day we remain close friends. I was at my Dad's shop where he had dropped me off that morning (I only had my learning permit at that time and wasn't driving myself yet).

I remember that day like it was yesterday: The knock on the door and seeing Jamo. I asked him what he was doing there, and that's when he broke the news to me that I was never going to see my mother again. Now it might sound strange that your friend knew your Mom had died before you did. But looking back on it I wouldn't have had it any other way.

It's a rare thing to have a friendship with someone for 35-plus years. Jamison is like the brother I never had. Relationships come and go, but I know this friendship will be always and forever. Love ya, Jamo! Senior year of high school was no cakewalk, but I had a different perception or mindset than the anger, bitterness and resentment I displayed in my junior year. After I graduated from high school and took a brief mission trip to Mexico, I went into the working world, as I had no desire to go to college. Jamison had no interest in college either, and we both started out as laborers in the construction field.

Jamison excelled at it, and worked his way up and now owns his own construction company. As for me, the heart and motivation were there, but the speed wasn't. I struggled mightily in the construction field. I remember that during that timeframe in my life, my favorite part of the day was the seven hours I would sleep. Have you ever felt this way, that you just wanted to get away from your life, and sleep was the only escape? It was no way to live, and the misery, lack of confidence and feeling of failure I felt before arose inside of me yet again.

Opportunity #1

Friends of mine and members of my church saw how this was eating me up inside at 19 years old. Thankfully an opportunity arose that was presented to me, and I chose to capitalize on it: Selling at flea markets. I knew nothing about sales. But being 100 percent Italian, no one would ever mistake me for the quiet kid on the block. My Dad would later say that I had sales in my blood, as he sold Electrolux vacuum cleaners – Google it, Millennials – door to door as a part-time job before I was born. My Dad taught me a lot, but I'm not sure I can give him credit for this one. Sorry, Pop!

Anyway, back to my journey of flea market sales. I would pack up an Iveco box truck late at night and get up 4:30 a.m. to drive up to two hours away to set up my stand. I'd put out my display of cushions and redwood furniture. Later in the season it would be an assortment of fireworks and then Christmas trees.

To be successful in life and fulfill your potential 100 percent, every person needs to figure out what makes them tick, what they are passionate about, and how they can positively affect the lives of others. This was the start of that revelation for me even though I didn't have a clue how this would affect my life in the years to come.

I was learning how to talk to customers, and trying to figure out what makes others tick, communicating with them about the products I was offering and how they would benefit them.

Lastly, I learned the art of negotiation and how to go back and forth on the price, as everyone was looking for a deal at the flea market. This was real on-the-job training for me, and it was not easy.

I remember early on learning the hard way that taking checks was very risky (this was before digital phone credit card readers). It didn't matter how honest the person looked. Those checks can be and were as funny as a $4 bill. Not everyone in this world choses the straight and narrow path of honesty.

Despite the bumps in the road and life lessons I *needed* to learn, I absolutely loved doing this! It was the first time in my life that I felt like I was good at something. This gave me some much-needed positive self-esteem, confirmation that I was not a loser and a failure. I was able to make a difference in the lives of others and feel confident in what I was doing. This might sound like very normal feelings that most of you experienced right away, but this was a first for me. I felt like it was the pot of gold at the end of the rainbow or the silver lining in the clouds. I, Anthony Santangelo, was finally experiencing joy and happiness

Opportunity #2

Selling at flea markets is something I will always remember fondly. It was my first opportunity that I experienced success with. The only issue with selling at flea markets in Pennsylvania was I couldn't do it all year long. It was August of 1997, and I had just finished up a successful July with the fireworks. I had a rare day off from working seven days a week back then, and Jamison's parents, Pat and Joan Glennon, invited me down to their trailer that was near one of the beaches in Delaware.

Jamison was working that day, but I accepted and headed down to the beach. Pat and Joan are like family to me; I have known them since I was five years old, and they are always there for me. I knew I could squeeze in a few more weeks of selling fireworks until kids went back to school, but had no idea what I was going to do from September until late November, when Christmas tree sales would start up. I remember this like it was yesterday, walking the beach with Pat, side by side, asking him: What do you think I should do these next few months? It was then that he said to me: "Anthony, why don't you sell cars?"

I remember laughing my ass off at him. He said, what's so funny? I told him, those guys are scumbags! As soon as I said that, he grabbed my arm and made me face him. And then said to me: if those guys are like that, how much better would you be? Pat says many things that are full of wisdom, and this was as big as they get!

Anytime he says something wise, Pat gives a smile that is similar to the one Tom Selleck does in "Magnum P.I." and "Blue Bloods." Just minus the mustache!

He looked at me. I looked at him. Then I said, "OK, Pat, you have never led me astray in the 15 years I have known you, I will take you up on your advice." I was 20 years old.

So off I went looking through the *Philadelphia Inquirier* – there was no Indeed, ZipRecruiter, Craigslist or CareerBuilder back then, Millennials – circling car dealership ads and calling them. I interviewed at somewhere between 12 to 15 car dealers, and was told the same things time and time again: Sorry kid, you are too young. Why do you want to do this? This is an older man's job, and you have your whole life ahead of you. No experience, no job. On and on I heard rejection after rejection.

One thing about me is that when I get something in my mind – and Pat definitely planted that seed – *I don't give up!* I had an interview set up at a Volvo dealership. I remember sitting there with that sales manager thinking how much I really disliked him. I thought, even if they offered me employment, I was going to turn it down. I was so frustrated and ready to give up and head back home to apply to carpet cleaning companies (something I did in high school). Then I decided at the last second to walk across the street to another car dealership, just to see if they were by any chance hiring.

I walked into the Devon Nissan used car department and was greeted by Terry Biagi. He was the manager and it was his day off, but he was there to pick up his check (no direct deposits back then). I asked him if they were hiring, and he said yes. Amazingly, even though he had his young son Colin with him, he took the time to interview me.

He told me, I like you and want you to come back to meet with Joe Bush Jr. (of the family that owned the dealership) at 3 p.m. I happily agreed and was very excited. Terry didn't stereotype this 20-year-old kid. He didn't care that I had no car business experience. He looked at my motivation, commitment and heart.

I came back at 3 p.m., and Joey was busy so I interviewed with Jeff Marcus. Jeff would later tell me that he was impressed with how I was eager and willing to do anything to have an opportunity to sell cars. Jeff told me he would call me at 9 p.m. that night. I drove home so pumped and filled with excitement that you would have thought I won the World Series of Poker (more on this topic later...). I had no idea that the dealership closed at nine.

I called at 8:55 p.m. (it was a Friday), and was on hold for 10 minutes. I waited anxiously, praying that Jeff would pick up the call after hearing it announced on the PA system. He finally did and told me *I started on Monday!* All I could think was that my perseverance and *commitment* – this won't be the last time you hear this word from me – paid off, and how God was faithful!

On September 8, 1997, at 20 years old, I started my new career in the car business at Devon Nissan. I was nervous as can be when I met my new colleagues, all of them some 10 to 30-plus years older than I was: Roy, Mike, Joe, George, Chuck, Sherman, Greg, Eva, Christine, David, John, Paul, Murray (RIP. Miss you buddy) and Tommy (RIP. And the funniest man I have ever met in my life who I think about every week). I also met my management staff: Jeff, Terry, Leigh, Mark, Kevin, George (RIP. I will talk about him a little later) and Brian, a rookie manager that was only four years older than me. I was a sponge trying to soak up all the knowledge I could, especially from Brian, who I felt I could relate to as he was so close to me in age.

After two weeks of watching Joe Verde automotive sales and management VHS videos, I was told to get ready to take my first "up" – a term used for a customer. I was so excited and ready. Well, so I thought. I took customers and saw early on how selling $50 of fireworks in the Poconos was just a little bit different than selling a $20,000 car. I was scared, uncertain and afraid of failing. The kid that never shut up was afraid to talk to people, as I was convinced in my mind that only other young people would buy cars from me. I thought that a person two or three times my age wouldn't respect me enough to do business with me.

Here is a big but simple life lesson: If you think you can't, you won't; but if you think you can, you will. I was developing a stigma of being my own worst enemy.

I was holding my own with the big boys for my first few months. Then came my fourth full month in the business, January of 1998. I completely fell apart. I talked to 41 ups (customers) face to face and only sold two-and-a-half-cars cars! National closing percentage back then was about 22 percent. My closing was 6.1 percent. I thought for sure I was going to get fired. And walked around telling all my fellow salespeople this. Again, I felt like a complete failure and those suicidal thoughts from a few years ago were creeping back around.

The guys took me out, and said, come on Santangelo, we'll buy a beer. I said guys, I won't be 21 until next month, and I don't drink (still don't). Then they told me, we'll buy you a Coke and a cheeseburger, we know you like them (some things never change). They told me to hang in there, and that my managers Terry and Brian liked me. Instead of giving the kid the hook, they stuck with me.

The following month, I was the top salesperson and earned my first plaque on the wall! (Who says cheeseburgers are bad for you? They worked for me!) I started learning what it meant to earn customers for life by doing proper follow up. And earning a confidence that was deeper then any I had ever experienced before.

Dating

Between watching my Mom die, and playing/watching sports non-stop as a teenager, dating was something that I really didn't get involved with. Plus the girls I liked, I knew only wanted to be friends with me.

Then about seven months into my car sales career, I met a girl who I will refer to as "T" that I fell completely in love with. I knew she was the one, and we were engaged in October of 2000. I remember thinking that I was on top of the world. I was on my way to becoming one of the top salespeople at Devon Nissan, and I was able to get the girl of my dreams.

In March 2001, my world came crashing down as T ended our engagement. I was crushed and hurt in a way that I had never experienced before. This was a huge setback in my life as not only was my heart broken, but the number of cars I was selling started dropping.

All of us need mentorship and guidance in life, and I was very grateful to have a management staff at the dealership that truly cared for me. Leigh Timberman was my direct sales manager that I reported to back then. One day he pulled me out of training. He told me how he needed me to start selling the number of cars that he knew I had the potential to sell. He also wanted me to know how much he, the other managers, and the owners – The Bush Automotive Group – cared about me. They wanted to help me through this very difficult time in my life.

The Bush family actually paid for me to see a counselor who was a very loyal client of ours. For any dealer principals or owners of any business, let this be an example of how you should treat your employees. The Bush family and their management staff (George, Jeff, Leigh, Terry and Brian) cared about me both as a person and as a salesperson who made them money. I will never forget how privileged I was to start my career with an awesome management staff and ownership. I worked for two great owners over the majority of my career selling cars.

Thank you to Mr. Bush, Joe Bush and Dean Bush for giving me my start in my career and teaching me how to earn customers for life. Also thank you to Peter and Stuart Lustgarten for having the privilege and honor to work for you my last nine years selling cars at Concordville Nissan & Subaru. From the guidance I received I was able to get back on track again.

It was late 2001, and this is when I wrote something that I try to apply in my life on a daily basis and I teach in my training classes: "You can't change the past, only do what is right in the present to make a better future." I started to realize that I *needed* to stop living backwards. This had to do with personal relationships as well as how I related to my colleagues and clients.

If you make a mistake, *so what?!* Learn and grow from it. No one gets to any level of success in life without failures, trials and tribulations. One of my favorite quotes from my favorite fictional character is: "It's not how hard you can hit, but how hard you can get hit and keep moving forward." From The Italian Stallion, Rocky Balboa.

Over 19 years I sold 3,486 cars. I still occasionally go back into the trenches to sell a car or two to longtime customers of mine (Remember: customers for life). I also hold the record for most cars sold at Concordville Nissan & Subaru (this will be broken by my friend Anthony Cappello in the next few years) and the highest CSI (Customer Satisfaction Index). During my last five years in sales, my CSI was ranked in the top one percent in the country for Nissan North America. I don't want to paint a picture that this journey was easy, as it was far from that. It was a flat-out grind at times. But thanks to my mentors I was able to keep focused on my goals and tasks at hand to achieve success.

George DuBois was someone who always knew what to say to talk you off the ledge that we salespeople ofttimes find ourselves on. We worked together for several years, but I learned more from him during our phone conversations as he was driving his 60 mile commute home at night. He was always there for me, speaking words of encouragement when I was down and letting circumstances and others affect me.

A few of his favorite quotes were: "It's a marathon not a race;" "Don't listen those guys, they are grasping at straws;" "Sometimes you have to put the square peg in the round hole," and my personal favorite, "Sometimes you have to drop back and punt." It seemed like every time I spoke to George, the next day I would sell multiple cars and/or set up multiple appointments for the week, I learned so many things from him, and I know I wasn't the only one. Chuck Desantis and David Ginsberg feel the same way. George was our mentor and leader right up until his passing in March 2013. You should have seen the turnout for his viewing! Salespeople, both current and former, plus managers, owners, accounting personnel and others packed the small church in Bridgeton, NJ, where George grew up. Jeff Marcus, George's best friend, gave a touching eulogy. It was obviously a sad day. But also, in a way, a great one to see how many lives George positively affected in his too-short 49-plus years that he was with us. We all have a little of George that we carry inside us, and his legacy lives on. I miss you, my friend.

Marriage

I did move past my broken engagement, and after experiencing the good and bad times of dating, I met a lady that I will call "B." Again, I fell hard and we were engaged within eight months. I thought to myself she was exactly what I wanted. We were married on May 1, 2004.

On Memorial Day weekend the following year I was on a huge emotional high. I did a hat trick – sold three cars in one day – that Saturday, and went to a Kenny Chesney concert later that evening. It was an awesome holiday weekend until the next morning, when B told she wanted the big D!

I was shocked and did everything I could to keep us together. But we separated in June 2005, and I was officially divorced that November. As they say, hindsight is always 20/20, and this was a very valuable life lesson that I learned. It was that just because you look good in paper – both with solid careers, perfect credit, etc. – doesn't mean you are good for each other. This was different then my broken engagement. I started to realize that I still had a lot of growing up to do.

I struggled mightily with negativity back then, and it affected every aspect of my life. I remember one of my managers, Jeff Deren, telling me how he loved everything about me except my damn negativity. I took a hard look at this in my life. Even though I wouldn't fully overcome this issue until years later, I started working on things and changing my perception of life.

This was also from the help of my best friend David Ginsberg and his awesome wife Nicole. Your inner circle should consist of at least five people, and they have to be different in how they relate to you. You need to have those that you go to for support, and those that will kick you in the ass when needed. This is how we grow: by being challenged. And those that love us the most should be challenging us to be different, not trying to protect us from the unknown! It's also important to be humble, and even learn from those that you mentor (love ya, Farid Abumohor!). I tell my new hire recruits across the country week in and week out how I learn from them, and use what I learn to become a better sales trainer.

It's also important to be humble, and receive learning from those that you mentor.

The car business has been and remains a very rewarding career for me. Trust me from personal experience that there is nothing better than hearing from customers these two things: 1) This is the best car buying experience I have ever had; 2) I have never bought a second, third, fourth... twelfth car from the same person before! It's very humbling to be able to give a service to others in an honest and ethical way in a field that isn't always known for that. I have taken great pleasure in earning customers for life. Many of whom I have also become friends with.

I started in this industry in 1997 with just under $1,000 to my name. Now 99 percent of my net worth has come from the car business. The other one percent is from poker. When I am not in dealerships across the country, you will find me at the poker tables. I am a semi-professional poker player on the low-end stakes circuit. I have turned a profit for several years in a row now, and have been at the World Series of Poker the last three years. I am still looking for that big score. But as I teach in my training classes, it will require patience, mental commitment, financial commitment and the *time* commitment to achieve this success. I know I will get there by going *all in* with this philosophy and mindset.

I have done many things wrong in my career. One of them was being selfish and not helping others. I was like this for the majority of my career selling cars. The last six or seven years I began mentoring other sales-people. I started to change my ways, but still had a long way to go. I also refused to use text messages and Facebook (or what I liked to call Fake-book). My processes did work, but I flat out refused to adapt to change to experience greater success.

Bottom line: *I was wrong.* In 2015 I started to feel the need to branch out more and give back to others, so I opened a twitter account: @pokercar-guy. Yes, I mixed poker in with car sales, and they both involve reading people. Here's a tip for the salespeople that are reading this. Once you figure out what makes you tick as a person, your ability to read others will get stronger, and it will help you sell more of your product. It also helps at the poker table as well.

I started making short videos about sales and mindset. I received very little attention, and looking back at them – you can watch them on YouTube under The Poker Car Guy – I was pretty awful! My content was OK, but I was so serious! I needed to loosen up and and relax.

This is something my favorite manager Moe Laraki has been telling me since 2007. Relax, buddy buddy! Don't you worry, papa! I love ya, Moe, and still get a kick out of how you speak French, English and Arabic all in the same sentence!

It was now 2016, and I decided it was time to move on from the day-to-day sales operations of the car business. I made up my mind that I was going to become a national sales trainer – giving back to others the nuggets of wisdom my mentors taught me and sprinkling in a few nuggets of knowledge that I have developed along the way as well. I started applying for training positions, and the rejections began to come just like they did for me back in 1997: You are too young, we are not interested, check back with us in a few months, and my personal favorite, you never were the General Manager of a dealership, so you are not qualified! Just like how it took me going through dozens of dealerships until I found the right opportunity with the Bush family, it took me a while to find the right company that would hire me as a trainer.

Opportunity #3
AutoMax Recruiting & Training

Even though I still refused to text and use Facebook, I was much a fan of LinkedIn, thanks to my longtime customer and now good friend Suzette Webb. I saw a listing on LinkedIn for a National Sales Recruiter & Trainer. It said to send your resume and a three to five minute video of me talking about anything. I had already made one where I spoke about how to make $100,000 a year in the car business. So I sent it to Ernie Kasprowicz, the GM/Partner at AutoMax.I was already connected on LinkedIn with Craig Lockerd, the founding owner and President of AutoMax, so I decided to send him the video as well. I apologized to Craig in advance if it came across like I was disrespecting the chain of command. He graciously understood and messaged me *promptly* to say that Ernie would call me the next day.

Over the next few weeks I had several phone interviews with Ernie and one with Craig, but never met them. They were more interested in how I communicated over the phone. This was probably a good thing as I told both of them that all I have to offer them is honesty and efficiency, as I have no good looks. This was something that I told my clients over the phone for years which always made them laugh. Well, Craig laughed and Ernie chuckled, and I was welcomed aboard as the newest National Sales Recruiter & Trainer for AutoMax.

I eventually met Craig as he did my trainer orientation. I started to discover that AutoMax was about giving opportunities to others, never touching dishonest dollars, and wanting to positively affect every person they come in contact with. I was right where I belonged, and I am proud to be apart of the AutoMax team.

Who is AutoMax? We are AutoMax! One of my assignment was to read a book by Og Mandino called "A Better Way to Live." This book talks about Og's life story and also provides 17 rules to live by. Rule #10 is called Dead at Midnight.

It reads: "Beginning today treat everyone you meet, friend or foe, loved one or stranger, as if they are going to be dead at midnight. Extend to each person, no matter how trivial the contact, all the care, kindness, understanding and love you can muster, and do it with no thought of reward. Your life will never be the same again"

I felt very guilty when I read this and thought how many times I treated people the wrong way: Cursing them out in traffic, copping an attitude in a store because that 17-year-old cashier was taking a long time in my eyes (when it was her first week on the job). Now when it was my turn to check out she had to deal with this attitudinal jerk of a guy. Plus airport personnel, hotel clerks, waiters/waitresses.... The list goes on and on. What if we treated everyone we met like they were going to be Dead at Midnight? Would this world be a better place?

Wouldn't car salespeople – not just men as the industry needs more women – sell more cars if they applied this principle and didn't judge books by their covers? These are a few things that I have the privilege and honor to teach in my training classes at AutoMax.

I have also made and welcomed the adjustments I needed to make and started texting and using Facebook. I see now how wrong I was, and how it stunted my growth not just as a salesperson but as a human being. You now will see me on Facebook Live a few times a week with my new hire recruits. You wouldn't be reading this chapter right now if I wasn't on Facebook, where I was discovered and asked to write this chapter because of my social media presence.

So I ask you again: do you achieve success in life because of luck, skill or mindset? Well, it's mindset every day of the week and twice on Sunday. It starts with the mental commitment that, yes, I believe in myself and I *will* accomplish my goals! Followed by a financial commitment that you will invest in yourself to achieve the level of success you desire. Lastly, there's the time commitment of *never giving up!* And understanding that the trials and tribulations that you will experience will make you a better person as long as you stay focused on your tasks at hand by going *all in* every day of your life!

Anthony Santangelo has been in the car business since 1997. He sold 3,486 cars in his career and was ranked in the top one percent of the country in Customer Satisfaction Index from 2012-2016. He is currently a National Sales Recruiter and Trainer for AutoMax. His passion, integrity and work ethic are second to none, which shows in his goal of positively affecting everyone he interacts with in becoming a better person.

Anthony is committed to following his life cycle every day, which consists of learning, developing, growing and teaching. This applies not only to the car business but in his personal life as well. In his free time, Anthony is an avid sports fan and semi-professional poker player.

Chapter Four

The Mindset Steps to Success

Joao Rios

L ooking back, I can clearly see the day I began my journey. I awoke very early – around 6 a.m. – filled with anticipation. It was a sunny morning like many others in Minas Gerais, a state in Brazil's outback, and the nearby scent of green grass combined with the dazzling view of the sun rising up in the mountains took the place of the clamoring sound of cars and horns that usually poured through my window. What an unfamiliar feeling for a boy who had been raised in the big city of Belo Horizonte.

That day was to prove very important to my future because I was set to close my first transaction in the cattle business with a man called Tunico, one of my mom's friends. Although I wasn't really sure what I was doing, something inside me insisted that I was heading in the right direction.

At just 16 years old, I didn't have much money, but I had put aside all that I had saved and borrowed enough from my mom to buy two or three cows. My hope was to keep them on our farm for a while and, once they got fatter, sell them in the marketplace. None of my friends were doing anything like that. In fact, they didn't even know what I was doing, and I didn't try to explain it to them because no one I knew at that time would have understood the concept of spending money today to get more money back tomorrow.

A couple of months later, it became obvious that my experiment had failed. This first transaction turned out to be a disaster for a couple of reasons, not the least of which was the fact that the market value of my cows had decreased during that time, so I lost money on my very first investment experience. Not a good beginning.

Almost three years passed, and there I was again, doing what nobody else in my circle of friends or family were doing – investing money in the present and looking forward to making more money in the future. This time, I was a 19-year-old boy investing my hard-earned savings in the stock market, and not very clear about what I was doing. The only thing I knew for sure was that I was determined to find another approach to life – a different way to make money, a surer way to achieve success in life.

To sum it up, I failed again. I invested all my money in the stock market and lost it all! At 19 years old, I had tried twice and failed twice. This was my second defeat. I had lost all of the money I had worked so hard to save… and now I had to start all over again.

My purpose in writing this chapter is to show you how the 10X Mindset has changed my life. Our mind is a very powerful tool, and we can use it on our behalf or against ourselves. It is vitally important to learn to control our mind and use it to work in our favor.

Stay with me. I will show you how I was able to use the 10X Mindset to improve my life and keep focus on what is important to me. I do want to state that my life is still a work in progress. I am not in a position to give you any advice. However, I can share with you what I have been doing and how these actions have been helping me. And then you can judge by yourself if it makes sense for you or not. The most important thing is to have a clear picture of your ultimate goal, and understand that the only thing that will move you from thoughts to reality are the actions you take today.

I have been engaged in active pursuit of my dreams for many years, and through this process, I have learned many things. I have connected with amazing people whom I would never have imagined I would be able to meet. Once you start, you will see things happen at light speed, and your life will transform completely. People around you will be astonished to see what you will become.

In the following pages, I will share a little bit of my own journey, including lessons I have learned and times I have failed. During our journey together, I will share with you the three main habits that helped me to achieve the 10X Mindset, and to realize some of my dreams.

The first element of change is awareness. Your first step is to be aware of the situation you are in now and to have a clear picture of where you want to be in a few years. However, simply being awakened is not enough. The only way to change your reality is through taking action. People often get stuck right here, but believe me, if you refuse to take chances, you won't achieve anything. As Brad Lea says, "You have to take a chance. Take action." Grant Cardone says, "Commit first and figure it out later." When you start taking action, things start to happen and your life begins to change.

Triggers

As we start our journey, the first step I took is to identify: What are my triggers? Do you know what yours are? What is your purpose in life? Why do you want to be successful?

When I first started to do this exercise, I thought my purpose in life was just to be successful in the industry I have chosen, or just to be wealthy. Later on, I realized this was not my purpose, not even close. Achieving success is great, but this is not your why. Find your why and the how will appear.

Most people find that their real purpose is to help other people, to help their families, or to impact the world in a positive manner, and that is great! Being successful and possessing money and power will enable you to achieve your dreams. Remember: you can't help anyone if you're in need of help.

First, get your own issues straight; then, you can look outward and begin helping others. Find your purpose. I always think about where I want to be three years from now, and then I do reverse engineering to figure out what I can do today that will move me toward my future goals. Every decision I make in my life is based on the answer to one question: "Am I moving toward my goals or away from them?"

Step One: Be Aware – I'm thinking back a couple of years to when my pursuit started. The first trigger I recognized in my life was generated by a book many of you certainly know called "Rich Dad, Poor Dad." My mom gave me a copy of that book when I was around 15 years old, and what I learned from it completely changed my life. That book brought me awareness and, at the same time, it triggered my deeper feelings and planted the seeds of my growing interest in personal development and international business.

As I read the book – and I strongly recommend that you read it plus give a copy to a close friend or family member – I realized that you can decide what you want to be and what you want to achieve in life depending on the effort you are willing to put in.

Step Two: Find Something You Are Passionate About – This step is very important, and it will be an essential focus in the next part of this chapter. You need to find something you are passionate about and learn everything about it. What is your passion? You might already know. Or you may need to give it some thought. For you, it could be sales, internet marking or real state.

For example, I am passionate about foreign trade. I help companies export and import products, and this involves topics such as international business, international logistics, marketing, sales channels, cost analysis and so on. I have accumulated a vast body of knowledge about all these topics. When you like something, you must research every aspect of that topic, and eventually become an expert. Do that right now. Grab a blank sheet of paper and start a list of topics you're interested in. Then select the topic that captures your interest most strongly.

Triggers make you rethink life the way it is, or the way people want you to believe it is. When I read "Rich Dad Poor Dad," I came to realize that life could be different from the common sense of having a normal life. The most important thing you can do is develop awareness. In other words, become convinced of your position today and the position where you want to be in the future – going from point A (you today) to point B (what you want to achieve). The path between plan A to plan B is the way you must go through to arrive at the point B. This action you take during this time will determine how long it will take for you to arrive at destination.

There will be times when you don't feel motivated or you don't feel that you are as passionate to the topic you have chosen. This is normal, life is made of ups and downs. The most important thing is to keep the constancy. Do whatever you have to do even though you don't feel like it. Every day counts.

There are days that you wake up in the morning and you don't feel like doing anything. I remember one day when I was feeling exactly this way. I woke up, took a shower, ate breakfast, jumped into my car and headed for work. While I was driving, I took my iPhone out of my pocket and clicked on the music app. I was driving and trying to click on the music app, and I opened the Audible app instead.

Only God knows how, but when I clicked again, I heard a man talking. I was like, "Damnnn… I don't want to listen to this." But because I was driving, I couldn't stop and change it right away, so I had to listen. For the next five minutes, I listened to Brian Tracy reading his book "No Excuses" to me. What I heard was so amazing, and it touched me so deeply, that I listened to the whole book in three days. That book became my life's second trigger, and it came at exactly the right time. I had been feeling as if I was no longer moving toward my dreams. Instead, I was feeling empty and without a purpose. Have you ever felt like that? Yes – or yes? I bet some of you are feeling that way right now. That particular audiobook has awakened me again and again, and my personal growth and my professional life have both skyrocketed!

You must find your own triggers. I encourage you to spend time looking for mentors, reading books, going to conferences and seminars, and staying in touch with people who have a clear purpose in life. Keep pursuing your dreams and keep adding wood to your fire.

Step Three: Write Down Your Goals Every Day – One thing that has helped me keep myself focused along the way and to stay constantly motivated and fired up is one simple habit. I write my goals down every day, first thing in the morning and again last thing at night. If you like reading, I'm sure you've noticed many successful people talking about this. But the truth is that you will see (and believe) how powerful this is only when you start writing your own goals down on a daily basis.

Here's a perfect example: Jim Carrey wrote himself a $10,000 check at a time when he had only a few bucks in his bank account. He dated the check and kept looking at it for years, until one day he realized he was going to make it. How exciting is that?

Grab a pen and paper and just do it! Don't overthink your goals. Just write them down. Don't try to rationalize them. Don't be afraid to come up short, just write them down as they are now. I keep a legal pad beside my bed to write those goals every day. You will soon see that every time you write down your goals, you will get excited about them all over again. That will give you the motivation you need to take action, and to keep pushing until you reach your goals. If you do this regularly, you will be surprised at what you will become. I'm telling you, this is magic. Things will happen in your life.

Take Action

This is the most important step of the three I present in this chapter. Most people can find things that trigger them, but only a few can actually take the necessary action to change their reality. You might read a book, listen to an audio program or live through some situation in life that awakens you and brings back the dreams you once had – those dreams that have been kept in the back of your mind. The only way to transform your thoughts and dreams into your reality is to take action! If you never take any action, you will never be able to see your dreams materialize.

One of my favorite aphorisms says, "Thoughts lead to feelings that lead to actions that lead to results." It is important to understand this reality and accept that actions lead to results. If there is no action on your part, there will be no results. I know taking action can be difficult. Most of us have no idea where to start, no idea what to do, and no idea how to do it.

Step One: Take Action Today – I know that sounds weird, and might even seem irresponsible on some levels, but this is the Number One piece of advice I have been living by. We tend to take action only after we have everything figured out, or when we feel 100 percent ready. The problem with that approach is that we will never have everything figured out and we will never be 100 percent ready. Life is very dynamic. Something is always going on, and there will always be at least one factor that is not 100 percent clear. You have to learn to overcome barriers in life and take action without having everything figured out.

A very good friend of mine is the CEO of a start-up called RocketOn. This company is an interactive platform that connects coaches and mentors to clients worldwide. As a customer, you are able to browse through hundreds of profiles of coaches and mentors and pick the one you like the most. As a professional, you are able to connect with thousands of clients worldwide, and make money through coaching and mentoring them in your field of expertise.

I have been discussing this project with my friend for a while now, and I was giving him feedback and advice. I got so involved in the project that we concluded that having me as a shareholder would be valuable for the company. I joined the company as a shareholder even though I didn't have all the money to buy the shares at that time. Opportunities like this only come once, and by joining the company in an early stage I am able to help its growth and to grow the money I've invested. The bottom line is, sometimes you have to commit first and figure it out later, There will never be a perfect time for you to take action. The perfect time is now! We haven't launched to the mass public yet, but if you want to find out more about the company access it at: https://www.rocketon.io/.

My advice to you is: take action now! By now you know what you are passionate about, so go ahead and take action. Learn who the experts in your field are and follow them in every available social medium. Maybe you have an idea for a business you want to build. If so, go ahead and buy your online domain now. Enroll in a course that will make you more knowledgeable on your chosen topic. Let's go! The time is now!

Step Two: Be Persistent – Persistence is a quality present in most successful people such as athletes, businessmen and entrepreneurs. It means the continuance in a course of action in spite of difficulty or opposition. If we want to translate it to our reality it would be: to continue to do whatever you have to do in a daily basis in order to achieve your goal or dream, even though you can't see clear results yet. Once you are persistent and consistent the results will appear sooner or later.

I can see the trait in many of my customers. I help foreign companies export their products to the U.S. and American companies import/export their products from/to other countries. To be successful in this business you need to be persistent, because entering an overseas market will not bring immediate results.

I recently concluded a project with Brazilian companies wanting to export food to the U.S. Before we sold anything in America, we had to conduct a market research to find out if there was demand for the product we wanted to sell. We needed to understand the local market, the new competitors and what attributes the customers in the target market value – this might be different from the attributes of the customers in the companies' domestic market. Once we had done this, we needed to calculate the landed costs of the product in the U.S. after the international logistical process and import tax applied by the American government on the foreign products. Not to mention that the foreign companies needed to be registered with the American Food and Drug Administration, and they had to adapt the labels (to be in compliance with the FDA) and even the products (some of the products were too sweet for the American market).

This is a medium-long term project and it can take up to year to be concluded. The companies involved had to be persistent and kept doing what they knew they had to do to move forward with the project even though they were not selling anything at the time. Even more, they were actually investing money today in order to be successful tomorrow.

The companies that went through the entire process, respecting the timelines, had success in the American market, and now they are able to sell their products in Brazil and in the U.S, increasing their general revenue and profitability.

In addition to that, when the economy in Brazil is not doing well they can make up their sales by exporting more to the U.S., and when the U.S. in is crisis, they can focus more on the domestic market.

To sum up, the companies that are persistent and take action are able to create a competitive advantage over the ones that are not willing to go till the end. This is one of many proofs that clearly illustrate the point. When you follow these rules of action, good things will come your way.

Step Three: Put In The Work – This is the most important point of this chapter – put in the work. This is the difficult part, but it's where the magic happens. Are you willing to put in the work? Are you willing to sacrifice today for a better tomorrow? Are you willing to stay away from nights out with friends for a while and to work during the weekends? How bad you really want it?

If you are not willing to sacrifice your time for your goals and projects, then something is wrong. I have been working nights and weekends for more than two years now, even when I don't feel like it. Consistency is the secret.

As a matter of fact, you might have heard about the Hurricane Irma that hit a number of Caribbean Islands and the state of Florida in September 2017. The big concern about hurricanes, besides the destruction they can inflict, are the power outages they might cause. Entire cities and even states suffer from power outages for days or even weeks after a hurricane hits.

As soon as I learned that the hurricane was on its way to hit Florida, and most specifically Miami with a Category 4 or 5 strength, I decided to evacuate from Miami and go to a safer place up north to minimize the effects of the hurricane on my routine. I made this decision based in two factors: first security and second work. Yes, I couldn't afford being without power and Internet access for days or weeks. This would have caused major delays for my ongoing projects. One week is approximately 72 hours of work – 12 hours a day multiplied by six days – that I could not lose. Given these points, I made the decision to leave the city.

I contacted two friends of mine, and without hesitating we rented a house in Orlando where we would be safe and, most importantly, we would have electricity until things were back to normal in Miami. We drove to Orlando days before the hurricane was predicted to hit Miami. In Orlando, the dinner table was turned in a co-working station, where we each worked at least 12 hours a day. We had to stay in Orlando for exactly one week, and when we found out that the power had been reestablished in our neighborhood, we drove back to Miami.

While many people were actually happy to leave work and have a few days off, we were worried about losing one week of production. This is the type of commitment I have with my work, goals and projects. I am putting in the work now so I can get results in the future.

Never Quit

The most important trait of every successful entrepreneur is this: they never quit. No matter what happens – when they get hammered, suffer or struggle – they always remain present and positive. This is possible only because they believe in their results. They have a mission, and they never quit! They know it's true that you fail only if you quit. They hang in there until they fix what needs fixing, but they never give up. Keep this truth in mind: If you haven't quit, you haven't failed.

Step One: Overcome Your Fears – The number one reason you don't take action is fear. Yes, fear. You are afraid you won't be able to achieve the results you want, and this prevents you from taking action, and ultimately from achieving your goals and dreams. Remember, you only fail when you quit. If you hang tough, address what needs fixing and take massive action, you will not fail.

But what is fear?

Fear is the anticipation of pain. It means you're afraid of something that hasn't happened yet and may never happen. In truth, most of the things we fear never happen. Therefore fear exists only in your mind, and most successful people use fear as a green light, a motivator toward taking action. I take fear with me. Whenever I feel afraid to do something, I go ahead and do it.

For instance, in the midst of negotiating a big account or when I hesitate to cold call a specific company, I envision fear as a green light, pick up the phone and do what I have to do. Don't let fear hold you back; let it motivate you to take action.

Every time you move out of your comfort zone, you will experience fear! Your mind's goal is to keep you safely inside your comfort zone. However, your dreams and goals do not lay within your comfort zone or you would have already achieved them. You must leave your comfort zone and overcome your fear.

Why do you fear failing? What is your worst-case scenario? Grab a pen and paper and write down what holds you back. Describe the worst possible outcome of taking action. What is the worst-case scenario of cold calling, opening a business, expanding your business, spending money on that conference? Putting it on paper will show you that it's not so bad.

The worst-case cold calling scenario is having someone hang up on you. So what? Maybe the worst part of opening a business is debt in the bank. So what? It is not that bad. As Grant Cardone says, "It's not like you will die from it." Be willing to risk small things to achieve big things.

Step Two: Don't Be Intimidated – Don't be intimidated. Trust yourself. Put in the work, and I have no doubt you will succeed. Follow the steps above – find your why, find your purpose, invest in education, and learn everything you can in your field – and you will become an expert. People will come to you for solutions to issues nobody else can solve. Do the work.

I opened my first import/export business in Brazil at only 22 years of age. My partner in that business Fernando and I were attending the same college, and he is still my partner today. At 22 or 23, you don't really know what you are doing. But I knew I wanted to do what nobody else in the market was doing.

I had accumulated some import/export experience while working in this field since I was 18. We opened this business by renting a small room and buying furniture and a computer. Once more, I invested all my money in a business. At the time, Fernando and I were attending a class in international negotiation led by a professor who was an export consultant for a Brazilian cosmetics firm. Their goal was to export products abroad into another market.

Fernando and I always arrived early and were the last to leave. I remember asking our professor every possible question about exporting cosmetics and finding importers in other countries. We collected all the information we possibly could and put in the work researching much more. A couple of months later, we put materials together and went to the market in search of another cosmetics company willing to export its products. When one manufacturer expressed interest in working with us, we presented the export plan we had designed. Even though we had no previous practical experience, we had done our homework and made the effort.

That company accepted our proposal, and we put our export plan into operation. When you prepare and put in the work, things will happen for you. We were two young professionals with very few results to show a prospective client. I don't really know why this businessman hired us, but I think he noticed that we were willing to spend our days and nights to make things happen – and that is exactly what we did. We worked hard and researched everything available. Then, almost a year later, Fernando traveled to the Middle East to sign our first contract with a company that wanted to distribute Brazilian cosmetics in the Middle East. We signed that contract and started sending the merchandise. At that time, the value of each container of products was about $200,000, and we made a 10 percent commission! Don't be intimidated. Commit first and put in the work!

Step Three: Share Your Message – As Russell Brunson says, "Your message has the ability to change someone's life. The impact that the right message can have on someone at the right time in their life is immeasurable." In the same way that Brian Tracy and Grant Cardone changed my life, you can change someone else's life. I might change your life with this chapter in this book. All we need is a click. Become an expert. Accumulate knowledge. Make yourself the go-to reference in one field. Teach people and share your message.

Nowadays, we must have an online presence or we will lose value year by year. The world is changing, and online marketing is growing rapidly. Some YouTube channels have more audience and impact than some TV channels. Twitter has more exposure than some kinds of media, and well-written blogs garner more views than many printed media. Explore the online world and do so in a positive way.

Make sure to share valuable content with your audience, share your journey. Even though you might not be the most famous name in your industry, most likely the content you are sharing will affect your audience in a positive way – by giving them either the drive or the knowledge to do something in a better way than they are doing it now. Do this with constancy and learn how to brand your company, your product and yourself without being annoying.

Conclusion

By now you may feel a bit overwhelmed, and I understand that. I've presented a lot of material. The concepts I've shared are the ones I use every single day of my life. Identify Triggers, Take Action and Never Quit.

I've also included many action steps. Information is good, but you will produce results only when you put what you know into action. You must climb one step every day of your life. It has changed my life dramatically. Although I am still far from achieving my ultimate goal, I am in a constant state of development, getting better each day. One of my goals for this chapter is to share my message with you so you will know that, while I'm out there every day fighting for a better life and trying to do things in the best way possible, you can do the same.

If you want to follow my journey, I invite you to follow me via social media. I will be glad to talk with you and exchange information to help you toward your successful growth.

Follow me on Instagram: @joaofrios; Facebook: Joao Rios; and Twitter: @joaofrios.

To sum up, the most important thing is to have a clear picture of your dreams and understand that action is what will move you from thoughts to reality.

Joao Rios is a business executive with 12-plus years of experience in international trade, import/export and sales. He studied International Business in Brazil and International Economy at Columbia University in New York, and proceeded to work in a dynamic and complex environment of international trading and import/exports.

He has International experience in managing and dealing with customers and suppliers in

Brazil, Germany, the U.S. and China. He has helped companies to internationalize and to export their products into the United States. He has also helped American companies to export products and services abroad.

Chapter Five

Tips for Developing an Unstoppable Mindset

Spencer Davidson

Hey you. Yeah, you. The one reading this book right now. You have gotten this far, so one more chapter isn't going to hurt. Why did you pick up this book anyways?

Have you always wanted to be an entrepreneur? Are you someone who has a great idea but just not sure how to get started? Or maybe you own a local company and you want to expand. Possibly you're someone who has big dreams and visions but unfortunately the only support you're getting is through books like this one. Well, whatever your reason, I am glad you are here. Yeah, right here reading these very words.

So will what I have to say make you a millionaire? Help you get famous? Probably not, because I am neither of those things yet. But what I can share with you from my many ups and downs throughout life is something you won't learn by going to school, or even from your parents. What I am about to share with you is how to get the way you think, dream and envision to a level that is unstoppable.

Growing up for me there was a lot of change. I attended six schools, and the first time since second grade that I went to the same school for consecutive years was not until my sophomore year of high school. My parents went through a nasty divorce when I was about 12, and that affected a lot of things.

I went from living in one of the nicest and biggest houses in the neighborhood to moving into my best friend's house and sharing a room with him and my older brother (my friend and I were 14; bro was 16). There were just so many pieces that my dad had to deal with that it was the best solution.

He always tried putting my brother and I in the best situation to succeed in athletics, and would always tell us that we can be anything we want to be as long as we put in the work. While bouncing around from school to school, the only thing I really cared about was playing basketball. It didn't matter what color jersey I wore or the team's name across the chest. No matter what had happened that day at school or the drama going on at home, whenever I stepped onto that court the only thing that mattered was winning the game and nothing else.

Finally, when I got to high school things started settling down. At least I thought they would. I was hitting my peak in my athletic career and started drawing attention from college coaches on the basketball court. I was going into my junior year and had just got done killing it on the court all summer. I got my three-point shot down and I would always get a decently-sized small crowd watching me dunk in warm ups (they couldn't believe a white kid barely standing at 6 foot jumping like I could at age 16).

Unfortunately on the first day of practice in my junior year of high school basketball, I went for a dunk, and when I came down I felt the worst pain I've ever felt in my left knee. At the time I didn't know what the fuck happened, but I obviously didn't tell anyone because basketball was the only thing I cared about. So I bought as much Icy Hot liniment as a 16 year old could afford and tried ignoring the pain. I played my whole junior season of high school with this pain.

By the end of season I lost all my athletic ability and was popping two ibuprofen in the morning to just get through the day at school, then two more before the game along with applying Icy Hot three times a day. I went from being able to dunk off two feet and two hands the summer before to not even being able to touch the backboard. Fortunately, I was able to still average around 20 points a game because I got to the free throw line a lot, and my jump shot started coming around, so my dreams of playing Division 1 basketball were still alive... until that summer.

I had been playing in an AAU tournament – and still hadn't told anyone about the pain I'd been going through – and I was on a fast break. A year before the whole gym would've stood up to see a dunk. But this year I could barely get my foot off the ground, and that is when my knee just gave out and I went down. There were probably 100 college coaches in that gym. Not all of them were watching my game, but it sure felt like it.

A couple of weeks later I went down to Iowa City and had the surgery, and couldn't practice or play until two weeks before the first game of my senior year. Which basically meant any chances of playing Division 1 basketball were over since I couldn't finish the AAU circuit and wouldn't be able to get back to the athletic ability I once had. By the time I was able to put my school's jersey back on for my senior year, knowing I would only be playing the 20 some games left, I just wanted to forget it. Not just because my dream had been crushed, but I had also been going through some shitty off the court stuff that no one really knew about.

The school I attended was a football school, and if you didn't play football you were a "bitch, pussy or a fag." Well I didn't play, but what really pissed everyone off was that I did play my sophomore year and started varsity, but ended up getting hurt (surprise surprise) and was lucky to be able to play basketball my sophomore year. So when fall came around junior year and it was time to put on the shoulder pads, I said, "Fuck that," and took the time to go visit colleges for basketball. This really pissed off some of the other players and a couple of coaches.

I got bullied hard that year, kids calling me "pussy, bitch, fag," whatever. I could handle it. In one ear and out the other. So what if I wouldn't get invited to any of the parties, no big deal. I didn't want to risk getting caught anyways. The only thing I focused on was getting that basketball scholarship. So I spent a lot of time with someone who I thought could help get me there.

He was one of my basketball coaches. Not only did he help me with my game athletically, but he also helped me out with my academics, which wasn't really a strong suit of mine. I would spend my time during study hall in his room, watching game tapes, and time after school before practice doing my homework or studying for an upcoming test. For others, it didn't sit well with them. They thought that was the reason I played a lot. (It had nothing to do with the fact that my whole life I traveled across the country to play against some of the best competition like Andrew Wiggins, Tyus Jones and Jahlil Okafor, who are all now in the NBA.) And the thing was that I had asked for the help with my grades and always wanted to improve on the game. I knew what it took to get to the next level, and I needed all the help I could get. I also lived 20 minutes away from school, and he would give me rides to school and back home sometimes because I lost my license from a curfew ticket (from the one party I did go to, where I had a crush on a girl).

So now that I caught you up to speed, where were we? Oh yeah, senior year. In the middle of senior year during basketball season, my dad called me on my cell phone to tell me that we needed to sit down with the athletic director of my school (who was also related to the football coach).

I remember this moment like it was yesterday. The athletic director looked at me and asked if there was anything going on between me and my basketball coach. I was confused, like, what? Apparently there were rumors going around amongst kids and other coaches that my male basketball coach and I were having sex in his classroom after school. Fucked up, right?

That is when I blew up and said everything that was bottled inside of me for years. The athletic director then stood up and pointed a finger in my face and started cussing me out in front of my dad. Bad choice. To paint a picture of my dad, he is about 6 feet 2 inches and some 250 pounds of muscle. I thought he was going to knock the guy the fuck out. But instead he got up, we stormed out, and they got a letter from our attorney the following week.

All of this happened to go on during one of the greatest basketball seasons the school had ever seen. We were undefeated and ranked #1 in the state. My game was unstoppable, averaging nearly 20 points a game and shooting around 50 percent from the field, and just about to reach my 1000th point of my career. All of this going on was confidential, so no one knew all the shit that was going down. By the end of the season in our last conference game I scored my 1000th point. (Dropped 27 that night.) Not only did we win that game but we won conference. That game was away, and right after I got into a car, drove two hours, and the next day spent all day in mediation (court, basically). Then drove back that night, missed practice, and had a game on the next day, a Saturday. We lost to a team that had only won like four games a year. I was exhausted physically, and mentally I was just over it. I was over everything, even life at one point (thought maybe suicide was the way to go).

A couple weeks later we lost in the second round of the playoffs, I missed the game winning shot, and I cried all night. They weren't tears of sadness that the game I loved for 18 years was over, but tears of relief that I could finally put down that school's jersey forever. (Don't get me wrong; going to state would have been kick ass, but I was OK with being done.

That May was one of the happiest times of my life. I graduated from high school, had just settled the lawsuit, and was getting ready to move 1,000 miles away. I was headed to Breckenridge, CO. What for? Well I hung up the basketball jersey in exchange for an apron. Yep, you heard me correctly.

You see, all the late nights at the gym, the thousands of shots put up, the "doing whatever it takes to win" mentality on and off the court grabbed attention and opened another opportunity for me. The coach that helped me out all those years in the classroom and in the gym retired the same year I graduated. His lifelong dream was to move to Colorado and retire, except that he wanted something to stay busy, so he decided to open a coffee shop franchise. Well, he needed a manager and he knew that I was a hard worker, so he offered me the job.

At the age of 18 I would make $60,000 working for him, but trust me, I earned every cent I was paid. I thought I knew what sweat equity was by putting endless hours into the gym every day growing up, but I really didn't.

I put in 100-plus hours a week for months straight, no days off. to make sure that place ran smoothly. I did everything from ordering food to payroll to hiring and firing to making lattes with hearts on the top. I didn't necessarily love the work, but I started to love the idea of business, and the fire that I hadn't felt in my belly since the game I once loved came back. I would love seeing customers come into my shop instead of the Starbucks across the street. I loved seeing my bank account grow and being rewarded for the work I was putting in. I started noticing the million-dollar mountain homes and the $100,000-plus Range Rovers everywhere, and I wanted all of those things. I started reading and studying millionaires and billionaires in every industry.

Then one day I left it all. Why? Well for a couple months there I got burnt out, I was fucking tired, and to be honest I was in love with a girl. I got caught up in that life for a couple of months and moved back home to be with her. (She was the girl I had a crush on at that party that I mentioned earlier.) A few months later we broke up and I moved on.

I still had the big dreams and visions of becoming a multimillionaire, hell even a billionaire, so I was trying to find the best way to get there. That is when I came across the one and only Grant Cardone. I saw one of his YouTube shows called "Young Hustlers," and it happened to be the episode on why college is not necessary to be successful. I had been watching this video on my phone during my economics class I had been taking at the local community college.

I wasn't sure what path I wanted to go down, so I took a couple classes while I figured it out. Well, I figured it out in that very video. I put my phone in my backpack and walked out of the class and never looked back. Yeah, thats right – I dropped out.

I went home and did some research on Grant and saw that he had made it in sales. So I got on the computer and searched on Indeed for sales jobs in Des Moines. (I needed to get away from that town where I had gone to high school, yet this was still close to family, about two hours away). I found a job selling real estate, went down and interviewed, and got hired in June, had my license in August, and sold my first home 20 days later. I worked for that company for about seven months, then decided I wanted something better and partnered up with one of the best agents I knew, and we started our own firm. (He did everything I joined later, haha). And things have never been better – financially, mentally, and I am just so damn happy.

So how did I go from the worst years of my life to now some of the best? From suicidal thoughts to now waking up every morning with the biggest smile on my face? Well, now I will share with you what got me through those tough times and now what has me going through the good times!

Spencer's Tips for Mental Success

1) The Ability to Adapt Your Dreams

Now this may sound cliched or whatever but hear me out. I believe that we all as kids have this mentality. For me, I wanted to be in the NBA. I would stay up late at night in the driveway pretending I was Michael Jordan, hitting the game winning shots. Unfortunately, when growing older, genetics weren't in my favor. Barely standing at 6 feet tall and playing against some of the best talent in the world, reality set in a little bit.

So now my dreams were to play Division 1 basketball instead. A free education possibly, and maybe even play in the March Madness tourney! Well we all know how that turned out. So now what? I adapted again.

Now I dream of having a billion dollar empire. Not only growing my company across the country, but also succeeding in real estate investments. I dream of having houses in Miami and Colorado, and a *huge* mansion back here in Iowa (money goes a lot farther here). When I drive my 2016 Ford Focus to work, I will look down at my steering wheel and see a Ferrari or Rolls Royce symbol for a quick second until it fades back into that blue Ford symbol.

So what am I saying here? Give up on your actual dreams you had when you were a kid? No, but I think some of us lose the ability to dream the older we get. We just say to ourselves: that could never happen to us. My dreams now are much bigger than they were when I was in second grade.. Think about it: I went from dreaming about being an NBA player to about owning an NBA team (like Mark Cuban). So be willing to Adapt Your Dreams!

2) In One Ear and Out the Other

As you read in the earlier paragraphs, this was potentially what saved my life. If you want a strong mindset this is vital. You need to be able to block out all the negativity that comes at you.

Everyone that tells you "you can't do that" or "that's impossible" or "be realistic" needs to literally go right in and out. Now in addition to this you can develop the skill to channel it for a second and use that as motivation to get up every morning to prove those motherfuckers wrong; well, that is just a bonus. You will hear many negative comments in your life, and those people that end up getting through those tough times and the negative times are the ones that can master this skill.

It won't be easy, but trust me, it will be worth it.

3) Surround Yourself With Others Who Have the Same Mindest

At the end of the day, if you can find others who have the same dreams, visions and goals as you, it will make it a lot easier to make your dreams a reality. If you are surrounded by naysayers and people that tell you "you can't do it," you will eventually break down and believe them. This could be anyone from your husband or wife to your parents and friends.

To make sure that I am surrounded with the right mindset, I literally took a piece of paper and asked them, what side are you on? Do you believe in me? Or not? It has made my life so much better.

Also if you do have problems finding these people that support you, go out and search for them. Example: Out of the thousands of people at the 10X Growth Con (hosted by Grant Cardone), no one that I talked to told me my dreams were unrealistic. In fact most of them told me I was not dreaming big enough! So if you have to take a week off to go to a conference that will help you get to this state of mind then *fucking* do it !

So why did I tell you all of this? For you to feel sympathy for me? Hell no. And if you are reading this right now and thinking, "Shit, that motherfucker has had a good life compared to what I have been through" – hey, I hear you. And again, I know there are many people out there that have gone through way worse than me and that is why I wanted to be a part of this book. I wanted to show you how I got through my many struggles and failures and maybe you can apply some of these tips to help you. I also am tired of seeing others give up on their dreams and settling for much less than their full potential. I don't want to see you 20 years from wondering, "what if?" We all have the ability to live our dreams that we have always wanted. We might just have to adapt them along the way.

Finally, the main reason I said yes to writing this is because I wanted to create awareness. The awareness of bullying in the educational systems. Not the typical big kid picks on little kid, who goes and tells a teacher, but the kids that are being picked on by the people that you are supposed to go to – teachers, coaches, etc. Who are we supposed to go to? No matter what happens in my life that is one thing that I will make sure stops. I am tired of teenagers ending their lives before they even begin. So whatever I have to do to make this happen I will do. And anyone telling me, "it's not possible," well, save your breath and get the fuck out of my way. Because one thing I have learned throughout the years is an unstoppable mindset, and honestly, *no one* can stop me because *I'm all the way up!*

Dedications/Shoutouts

I would not be where I am today without the following people in my life:

• My Brother (Tim): I appreciate you always being there and putting me before anyone else, even yourself. The shit you have gone through and bounced back from is truly amazing. You were the first person in this family to start a sales career and show us how rewarding it can be. We will do amazing things together and I can't wait to see what the future holds for us! #MillionaireBrothers

• Dave (Coach): I appreciate all the help throughout high school and the first years of my career. All the opportunities and hours spent working on my game or grades means a lot. I don't think I could have gotten through school without you. Enjoy the Rocky Mountain living!

• Andrew (My Business Partner/Friend): Thank you for believing in me and giving me the opportunity of a lifetime. Together we are unstoppable and soon the world will know that! #NectrRealty.

• Chase (Best Friend): Thank you for being my best friend since sixth grade. No matter how many schools I have been to, we just always seemed to remain best friends. I know sometimes we don't agree on certain things or butt heads on other things, but we can always talk it out, and I know you always will have my back. Thank you again for helping out with this chapter and always being there!

• Cindy and Doug Hahn (Aunt and Uncle:) You guys are truly the nicest, most caring, gold-hearted people I have ever met. No matter what I would do, you guys would support me 100 percent. You helped raise me ever since I was born and you still help me into early adulthood. I know it has not been easy throughout the years, but as long as we stick together we can get through anything. Part of what I do and why I do it is because of you guys, and I want you to know that part of the reason why I want financial freedom is to make sure you never have to worry again.

*Liz Davidson (Mom): Being a cancer survivor and showing your toughness through that has truly inspired me and has really put life in perspective and you have showed tremendous resilience in bouncing back and getting back on top with your career . Thank you for all your help as of late helping me get through some of the early entrepreneurial struggles.

• Tim Davidson (Dad): Being able to call you my Dad has been the biggest honor of my life. No matter what life put you through, you have not only persevered through it but you always put us kids first: The endless hours of time spent with me growing up playing sports, traveling across the country with me and coaching my tournaments. All the hard earned money you spent to make sure I always had the best equipment, shoes, etc. Sticking up for me when shit hit the fan at school. Always preaching to me the importance of money and becoming financially free. Life has thrown us a lot of curveballs but I finally see a chest high fastball coming at me and I am swinging for the fences and I will make sure you are with me every step of the way.

Chapter Six

Breaking & Making Habits Through Mindset

Alex Nava

" You have to break the bad habit, before the bad habit breaks you."
Alex Nava

I started smoking as a teenager, I thought it was cool to smoke and drink. But then it became an addiction. I became addicted to nicotine and I smoked for years and years and I became hooked to the smoking habit.

I tried quitting several times for years, but I couldn't quit. In the back of my mind, I knew I had to quit someday tough, but I wasn't sure how. Quitting seemed like a mission impossible, but I knew I had to break the habit or the habit would someday break me.

One day, I reflected on this: "you have to break the habit before the habit breaks you" and so just like that, I quit smoking. I broke the bad habit. It wasn't easy to do it, but I did it!

It took one decision, and I did it one minute at a time, one hour at a time, one day at a time, and those minutes; hours; and days seemed an eternity! I had the cravings; I would get hungry all the time; Many times I felt like I couldn't resist it; But I didn't want to go back and pick up the habit again because I had a commitment with myself. And I remembered my "why," and my "why" was "break the habit before the habit breaks me"

I agree with Grant Cardone; there is no such a thing as balance! How can you have balance when you smoke? I remember how I would smoke until my lungs would hurt. I was obsessed! I literally was on 10X mode on my smoking and drinking habit.

It is not easy to break a bad habit; It's a constant battle! But; I believe the key is to look at the benefits of the good habits and look at the disadvantages of the bad habits! If I do this, then I will get this or that, and we need to constantly remind our selves of the benefits and remember our "why" every day. For example, If I work out, then I will be fit and I would have more confidence, Or If I continue smoking, I will not have energy and I might contract lung cancer in the future.

Do you have a bad habit you are trying to get rid of? But you can't give it up? You are not alone; I've been there, and I know what you are going through; But you can break the bad habit before the bad habit breaks you!

You need to decide to quit; And once you make that decision to break the habit then you need to remember why you decided to quit! My "why" was: I didn't want the bad habit to break me, so I broke the bad habit instead!

Life has been better since I did. I have more energy and feel better overall. I am free of the smoking habit, and now I can't stand the smell of cigarettes.

I believe you can get rid of any bad habit if you make the decision to quit and remember your "why". Your "why" needs to be a strong "why" Otherwise you'll go back and pick up the habit again!

Why am I sharing this with you? The reason why because it is hard to have a good habit; when you have a bad one. You can't smoke and go to the gym; or run.

You get tired. And I don't know about you but when I was smoking or drinking I wasn't thinking about exercise.

You need to have the mindset of "yes, I can" Your mindset is key to sticking to the good habits! I am talking about reading, exercising, eating healthy, meditating; or whatever gets you closer to your goals and dreams. You can't become a positive individual if all your thoughts are negative! You need to get rid of whatever negative toxic habits. you may have before you can implement good habits and then become hooked on the good habits.

You need to ask yourself these questions: What am I doing this for? What am I getting out of It? What will happen to me in 10 years if I continue doing this? Everything we do will come back later as either a credit or a debit.

In most cases, what we do on a regular basis doesn't feel like a big deal now; But sooner or later the debit or credit comes back to us. The negative habits come back to us later in a form of a debit; A debit means a minus, a deduction to something, a deduction to our health, our finances, our business, our creativity, etc.

For example, after smoking for years, my health experienced a debit; I didn't have energy most of the time and I was lazy, I didn't feel like going to the gym and I would not go work out instead I would smoke a pack. All those actions we take day in and day out compound with time like money compounds with interest in the savings account as time goes by. Everything we do, either positive or negative, will compound with interest later, either negatively and/or positively.

It's not easy to get in a good routine because of challenges and commitments we have; But a good routine can make all the difference. When you see someone having success at something it's not an immediate success. They have been working at it day in and day out for years, and when they need to deliver they are ready! They crush It! They developed confidence along the way because of the actions they repeatedly took day in and day out! The key to experience new results and get hooked on good habits is to develop a good routine, like daily exercise, reading and thinking positive, and then make those activities "non-negotiables" Specifically, non-negotiable means to do it no matter what! You just do it! It becomes part of who you are! No excuses!

So what side do you want to collect from? The debit or the credit? I don't know about you, but I want to collect credits on a compound basis! The credits can be a better body, more energy, better health, better lab results, more money, more impact, more and better results.

You never know what program on TV you are going to watch or what book you will read or who you talk to, and out of nowhere out of nowhere something that is being said resonates with you and makes you see your reality! For me it was that simple phrase: "You have to break the habit before the habit breaks you" I think I heard that in a movie, I believe it was a Robert De Niro movie, but I can't remember exactly.

The name of the movie doesn't matter; what matters its that that simple phrase resonated with me and thanks to that I quit smoking and drinking.

 Funny how life works; You never know what will trigger something that can make a difference. But I know this- the more you stay connected with positive messages from books, movies, documentaries, audio books, etc. the better you are off because our brains need to have the daily dose of positive messages, and ideas; Otherwise we can become our own worst enemies. We can become easily attracted to the bad habits.

What are you going to do next? How are you going to spend your time? Who are you going to spend your time with? A lot of the time we know when we are not doing the right thing! We are secretive about It! We try to hide it from our friends and family because deep inside we know it's not the right thing.

Reflect and ask what this will do to you- in five years or in 10 years? Will I be around? Will the habit break me? Or will I break the habit? You can become victorious! You can become all that you can be! It only takes a decision and work. If you fall and go back to the old habit, just start again and start again! A lot of people quit completely because after a week or two they do it again and they say forget it, this is to hard I can't do it! But you need to start again, and again. You need to remember to be careful with the words you say to yourself on a regular basis because we pretty much believe whatever we say to ourselves. If we say we can then we can, if we say we can't, then we can't.

My mom always told me: " Quiero, puedo y hago!" Which translates as "I want, I can and I do". These words gave me confidence and helped me take risk and action.

These words resonated with me and I continue to say them when it gets tough!

My mom's magic words-, "Quiero, puedo y hago" helped me to get out of the "barrio" I grew up in Mexico.

I grew up in a poor and tough environment, and I used to hang out with the wrong crowd. I am lucky to be alive.

Some of the old friends I had there are still living in the same house and they are up to no good. One of my good friends couldn't break the drinking habit so the habit broke him. Rest in peace, David. We were young at the time and didn't know better. I knew I had to get out of that environment, but I also knew I could do more with my life. I decided to move to Los Angeles with limited money and limited contacts.

My Dad always told me growing up, "You have to go to school, graduate and get a good job" So my goal was to graduate from college. It was very hard being away from family and friends, even acting on the decision to move out was very difficult. I had to leave my family and dog behind.

But, I acted on that decision, and five years later I graduated from college with a bachelor's degree in Speech Communications. I was the first one in my family to graduate from College. I wanted to give up so many times because it was hard at times being alone and not having any family. But I remembered my "why" and my "why" was to graduate from college. I share this, because I believe that when you want something bad enough you can get it if you work hard at It!

It might get lonely on the way to your dream and it is a lot of work, but at the end it is worth it

I always wanted to have my own business, and now I have a successful insurance agency in Los Angeles, CA.

I have received many awards and I have been helping people with their insurance needs. I had many doubts in the beginning and many people told me it was hard to sell insurance. But you have to believe in yourself and take a chance.

I share this to let you know that you can achieve your dreams. You can get rid of the bad habits that have been holding you back! You can have a breakthrough and own that business, you can be helping and serving your community or go up the corporate ladder or be fit-. or become an entrepreneur-, or write a book, or become an actor, whatever your dream is, it can be done! Believe it can be done!

Life is not always easy, If you can find a mentor that can guide you consider your self lucky. If you don't have a mentor, get one. You can think of anything that can motivate you to push harder, work harder, etc. It might get lonely on the way to your dreams and it is a lot of work, but at the end it is worth it.

People try to scare you from doing what you want to do. They say it is hard and it is safer to stay where you are, where there is no risk and it's more comfortable. But you need to believe in yourself and take a chance. You can get rid of the bad habits, toxic people around you and whatever is holding you back! You can have a breakthrough.

Remember, stay connected to positive people and feed your brain with good stuff like a good book like this one. We need this type of stuff, especially with so much negativity around us.

Our habits are the key to help us accomplish our goals and dreams! Write down what you do at the end of the day and reflect on what you're doing; Is it getting you closer to your dream? If not change it! Are you spending time with people that are lifting you up or bringing you down? Are they helping you get closer to your dream? If not change your environment! Unless you are happy and content with who you are and where you are in life, then don't change anything!

Remember, the key to good habits is to make it a "non- negotiable " What does that mean? It means that no matter what, you will do it regardless. It is a non-negotiable, so you need to do it; And if you do it on a consistent basis you can reap the "credits" I talked about earlier.

Second, how bad do you want it? You build confidence along the way, God opens doors along the way! "(Help yourself and God will help you)" (Apply yourself.)

 Remember-, just decide and do it. You will find a way! I can say that I didn't become one more number of the crowd I grew up with, I got out of the negative environment, and I never went back. Do whatever it takes, burn the boats! Stretch yourself and reach out, put yourself out there! You can accomplish your goals! You can get rid of the bad habits and- adopt good habits, and believe me, you will collect the "credits" later!

When you don't feel like doing the things you know you need to do, think of your why! What would happen if you don't do it? What will you miss? Would you feel like you missed out if you don't try? Would you regret it later? Will you have a bigger bank account if you try? Will you be able to help others with your services? Will you experience a higher level of success? Higher income? What could happen if you don't try? Will you be happy? Will you be stuck at a job you hate? What's the worst thing it can happen if you try? What happens if it works? What happens if you make it happen? How would you feel?

In conclusion, remember that everything we do now counts, and we will either collect credits or debits. Remember credits are positive things we collect like more energy more money, more results and debits are lesser things we get to collect later. less energy, less activity, less money, etc. Every activity we engage in will give us a result. We know deep inside when we are doing something that is taking us further from our dream instead of closer. We know because we tend to hide it from our friends and family. When you get a routine of your good habits do them as often as possible. For example, I now make exercise a non-negotiable. I exercise three to four times a week, and I feel better and I have way more energy now than when I didn't exercise on a regular basis.

Take opportunities as they come, I never wrote a chapter for a book before, I am now glad I did. The first time the opportunity came by, I said no, but now I am writing it and I am glad I said yes. I am learning as I am writing this chapter. Maybe some of these words will help you to take action on writing a book you've been thinking about or taking on an opportunity for a new position at work, or maybe starting your own business.

Why not take a chance? What is the worst possible outcome that can happen if you take that opportunity? I tell you from experience that when I haven't taken a chance on an opportunity, I usually regret it later. I have more dreams to accomplish and more action to take on my business and in my personal life and right now I am seeing this book published and my name on the cover along with nine other risk takers, nine other individuals that are sharing their experiences with the world and are making a difference.

I could be watching TV or sleeping right now instead of writing; But as I do this I am pushing myself for the next thing, for the next dream to achieve, for the next chapter to write. This is even helping me commit to my habits.

Grant Cardone wrote the book "The 10X Rule" and he says to take massive action! Let's take massive action on our good habits today and collect credits later. He also says to do "whatever it takes". Do whatever it takes to stay on the right track and don't let anyone or anything keep you from attaining your dream

For me the habits that are helping me are exercise, reading, goal-setting, attending seminars, listening to audio books, watching what I eat, writing, praying and overall thinking positively, being thankful and being ready to help and provide value. It is not easy to do the right things when I feel a disconnect with my daily routines and habits. When I don't do the things I just mentioned I find myself ready to complain, blame and being negative. I believe it is easier to do my routine early in the day and it makes my day more enjoyable and more productive. It helps me deal with difficult people and it helps me confront the challenges of every day.

Your mindset is everything; If you think you can, then you can, and if you think you can't, then you can't. It takes the same energy to think negatively as it does positively. But when you think positively you get more done. Your mindset is crucial, keep reading, keep surrounding yourself with people with the same mindset.

Don't let others tell you that you can't or that you will never be successful. You can prove them wrong. Think positive no matter what, even if you are not where you want to be in life; Or if you are dealing with a bad habit you can't break, just try every day, one day at a time; If you fall, get back up and try again and feed your mindset with the necessary information to stay hungry and motivated. Look ahead and move forward. Advance little by little, and don't get frustrated if you don't see results. You have a better chance to succeed if you stay connected to your 10X Mindset, and your 10X habits.

Being connected to your 10X Mindset and habits really means to continue developing the "muscle" with massive and constant action.

I know it is not easy; It's a task, and every day challenge to do it; But remember that we are getting closer or further away from our goals and dreams through the actions we take every day. Remember to break the bad habit before the bad habit breaks you.! Do whatever it takes to get it done. Keep on challenging yourself to new levels and remember your "why". When we forget our "why" then we go backwards. If you fall, get back up and try again; Keep doing what you know you need to do to get yourself closer to your dreams.

I wish you the best in your journey to achieving your goals and dreams and remember "Quiero, puedo y hago"

"I want, I can, and I do"

10X Mindset and good habits are the key to get us closer to our dreams and achieving our goals.

Alex Nava has a Bachelor of Arts Degree in Speech Communications from California State University; He is married to Claudia and they have one son named Ethan.

- Alex has his own insurance agency located in Los Angeles, CA. He has been helping people with their insurance needs for 14 years strong, and Alex has achieved many awards and achievements during his career. Alex and his team are growing by helping individuals and businesses with their insurance needs

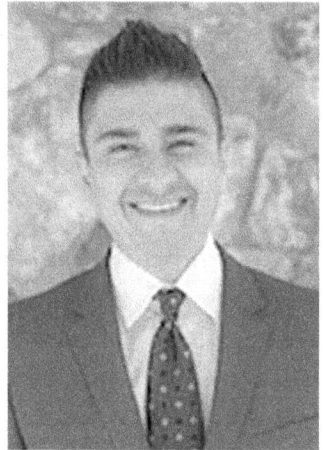

Daily Mindset Habits　　　　　Date _____

___ Wake Up Early

___ Morning Gratitude

___ Write Down Goals in Detail

___ Exercise (Walk, Run, Jump Etc..)

___ Read Something Positive

___ Pray / Meditate

Goals for the Month:

_____

_____

_____

_____

_____

_____

_____

_____

What Went Well (write down everything, no victory too small)

_____

_____

_____

_____

_____

_____

_____

Tomorrow's top 3 things to do

_____

_____

_____

_____

_____

Daily Mindset Habits   Date _____

___ Wake Up Early

___ Morning Gratitude

___ Write Down Goals in Detail

___ Exercise (Walk, Run, Jump Etc..)

___ Read Something Positive

___ Pray / Meditate

Goals for the Month:

_____

_____

_____

_____

_____

_____

_____

_____

What Went Well (write down everything, no victory too small)

_____

_____

_____

_____

_____

_____

_____

Tomorrow's top 3 things to do

_____

_____

_____

_____

Daily Mindset Habits   Date _____

___ Wake Up Early

___ Morning Gratitude

___ Write Down Goals in Detail

___ Exercise (Walk, Run, Jump Etc..)

___ Read Something Positive

___ Pray / Meditate

Goals for the Month:

_____

_____

_____

_____

_____

_____

_____

_____

What Went Well (write down everything, no victory too small)

_____

_____

_____

_____

_____

_____

_____

Tomorrow's top 3 things to do

_____

_____

_____

_____

_____

Daily Mindset Habits   Date _____

___ Wake Up Early

___ Morning Gratitude

___ Write Down Goals in Detail

___ Exercise (Walk, Run, Jump Etc..)

___ Read Something Positive

___ Pray / Meditate

Goals for the Month:

_____

_____

_____

_____

_____

_____

_____

_____

What Went Well (write down everything, no victory too small)

_____

_____

_____

_____

_____

_____

_____

Tomorrow's top 3 things to do

_____

_____

_____

_____

_____

Daily Mindset Habits   Date _____

___ Wake Up Early

___ Morning Gratitude

___ Write Down Goals in Detail

___ Exercise (Walk, Run, Jump Etc..)

___ Read Something Positive

___ Pray / Meditate

Goals for the Month:

_____

_____

_____

_____

_____

_____

_____

_____

What Went Well (write down everything, no victory too small)

_____

_____

_____

_____

_____

_____

_____

Tomorrow's top 3 things to do

_____

_____

_____

_____

Daily Mindset Habits Date _____

___ Wake Up Early

___ Morning Gratitude

___ Write Down Goals in Detail

___ Exercise (Walk, Run, Jump Etc..)

___ Read Something Positive

___ Pray / Meditate

Goals for the Month:

_____

_____

_____

_____

_____

_____

_____

_____

What Went Well (write down everything, no victory too small)

_____

_____

_____

_____

_____

_____

_____

Tomorrow's top 3 things to do

_____

_____

_____

_____

Daily Mindset Habits   Date _____

___ Wake Up Early

___ Morning Gratitude

___ Write Down Goals in Detail

___ Exercise (Walk, Run, Jump Etc..)

___ Read Something Positive

___ Pray / Meditate

Goals for the Month:

_____

_____

_____

_____

_____

_____

_____

_____

_____

What Went Well (write down everything, no victory too small)

_____

_____

_____

_____

_____

_____

_____

Tomorrow's top 3 things to do

_____

_____

_____

_____

_____

Daily Mindset Habits Date _____

___ Wake Up Early

___ Morning Gratitude

___ Write Down Goals in Detail

___ Exercise (Walk, Run, Jump Etc..)

___ Read Something Positive

___ Pray / Meditate

Goals for the Month:

_____

_____

_____

_____

_____

_____

_____

_____

_____

What Went Well (write down everything, no victory too small)

_____

_____

_____

_____

_____

_____

_____

Tomorrow's top 3 things to do

_____

_____

_____

_____

_____

Daily Mindset Habits   Date _____

___ Wake Up Early

___ Morning Gratitude

___ Write Down Goals in Detail

___ Exercise (Walk, Run, Jump Etc..)

___ Read Something Positive

___ Pray / Meditate

Goals for the Month:

_____

_____

_____

_____

_____

_____

_____

_____

What Went Well (write down everything, no victory too small)

_____

_____

_____

_____

_____

_____

_____

Tomorrow's top 3 things to do

_____

_____

_____

_____

_____

Daily Mindset Habits   Date _____

___ Wake Up Early

___ Morning Gratitude

___ Write Down Goals in Detail

___ Exercise (Walk, Run, Jump Etc..)

___ Read Something Positive

___ Pray / Meditate

Goals for the Month:

_____

_____

_____

_____

_____

_____

_____

_____

What Went Well (write down everything, no victory too small)

_____

_____

_____

_____

_____

_____

_____

Tomorrow's top 3 things to do

_____

_____

_____

_____

_____

Daily Mindset Habits　　　　　　Date _____

___ Wake Up Early

___ Morning Gratitude

___ Write Down Goals in Detail

___ Exercise (Walk, Run, Jump Etc..)

___ Read Something Positive

___ Pray / Meditate

Goals for the Month:

_____

_____

_____

_____

_____

_____

_____

_____

What Went Well (write down everything, no victory too small)

_____

_____

_____

_____

_____

_____

Tomorrow's top 3 things to do

_____

_____

_____

_____

Daily Mindset Habits   Date _____

___ Wake Up Early

___ Morning Gratitude

___ Write Down Goals in Detail

___ Exercise (Walk, Run, Jump Etc..)

___ Read Something Positive

___ Pray / Meditate

Goals for the Month:

_____

_____

_____

_____

_____

_____

_____

_____

What Went Well (write down everything, no victory too small)

_____

_____

_____

_____

_____

_____

_____

Tomorrow's top 3 things to do

_____

_____

_____

_____

_____

Daily Mindset Habits Date _____

___ Wake Up Early

___ Morning Gratitude

___ Write Down Goals in Detail

___ Exercise (Walk, Run, Jump Etc..)

___ Read Something Positive

___ Pray / Meditate

Goals for the Month:

_____

_____

_____

_____

_____

_____

_____

_____

What Went Well (write down everything, no victory too small)

_____

_____

_____

_____

_____

_____

_____

Tomorrow's top 3 things to do

_____

_____

_____

_____

Daily Mindset Habits   Date _____

___ Wake Up Early

___ Morning Gratitude

___ Write Down Goals in Detail

___ Exercise (Walk, Run, Jump Etc..)

___ Read Something Positive

___ Pray / Meditate

Goals for the Month:

_____

_____

_____

_____

_____

_____

_____

_____

What Went Well (write down everything, no victory too small)

_____

_____

_____

_____

_____

_____

_____

Tomorrow's top 3 things to do

_____

_____

_____

_____

Daily Mindset Habits   Date _____

___ Wake Up Early

___ Morning Gratitude

___ Write Down Goals in Detail

___ Exercise (Walk, Run, Jump Etc..)

___ Read Something Positive

___ Pray / Meditate

Goals for the Month:

_____

_____

_____

_____

_____

_____

_____

_____

_____

What Went Well (write down everything, no victory too small)

_____

_____

_____

_____

_____

_____

_____

Tomorrow's top 3 things to do

_____

_____

_____

_____

Daily Mindset Habits   Date _____

___ Wake Up Early

___ Morning Gratitude

___ Write Down Goals in Detail

___ Exercise (Walk, Run, Jump Etc..)

___ Read Something Positive

___ Pray / Meditate

Goals for the Month:

_____

_____

_____

_____

_____

_____

_____

_____

What Went Well (write down everything, no victory too small)

_____

_____

_____

_____

_____

_____

_____

Tomorrow's top 3 things to do

_____

_____

_____

_____

Daily Mindset Habits   Date _____

___ Wake Up Early

___ Morning Gratitude

___ Write Down Goals in Detail

___ Exercise (Walk, Run, Jump Etc..)

___ Read Something Positive

___ Pray / Meditate

Goals for the Month:

_____

_____

_____

_____

_____

_____

_____

_____

What Went Well (write down everything, no victory too small)

_____

_____

_____

_____

_____

_____

_____

Tomorrow's top 3 things to do

_____

_____

_____

_____

Daily Mindset Habits   Date _____

___ Wake Up Early

___ Morning Gratitude

___ Write Down Goals in Detail

___ Exercise (Walk, Run, Jump Etc..)

___ Read Something Positive

___ Pray / Meditate

Goals for the Month:

_____

_____

_____

_____

_____

_____

_____

_____

What Went Well (write down everything, no victory too small)

_____

_____

_____

_____

_____

_____

_____

Tomorrow's top 3 things to do

_____

_____

_____

_____

_____

Daily Mindset Habits   Date _____

___ Wake Up Early

___ Morning Gratitude

___ Write Down Goals in Detail

___ Exercise (Walk, Run, Jump Etc..)

___ Read Something Positive

___ Pray / Meditate

Goals for the Month:

_____

_____

_____

_____

_____

_____

_____

_____

What Went Well (write down everything, no victory too small)

_____

_____

_____

_____

_____

_____

_____

_____

Tomorrow's top 3 things to do

_____

_____

_____

_____

_____

Daily Mindset Habits   Date _____

___ Wake Up Early

___ Morning Gratitude

___ Write Down Goals in Detail

___ Exercise (Walk, Run, Jump Etc..)

___ Read Something Positive

___ Pray / Meditate

Goals for the Month:

_____

_____

_____

_____

_____

_____

_____

_____

_____

What Went Well (write down everything, no victory too small)

_____

_____

_____

_____

_____

_____

_____

Tomorrow's top 3 things to do

_____

_____

_____

_____

Daily Mindset Habits   Date _____

___ Wake Up Early

___ Morning Gratitude

___ Write Down Goals in Detail

___ Exercise (Walk, Run, Jump Etc..)

___ Read Something Positive

___ Pray / Meditate

Goals for the Month:

_____

_____

_____

_____

_____

_____

_____

_____

What Went Well (write down everything, no victory too small)

_____

_____

_____

_____

_____

_____

_____

Tomorrow's top 3 things to do

_____

_____

_____

_____

Daily Mindset Habits   Date _____

___ Wake Up Early

___ Morning Gratitude

___ Write Down Goals in Detail

___ Exercise (Walk, Run, Jump Etc..)

___ Read Something Positive

___ Pray / Meditate

Goals for the Month:

_____

_____

_____

_____

_____

_____

_____

_____

_____

What Went Well (write down everything, no victory too small)

_____

_____

_____

_____

_____

_____

_____

Tomorrow's top 3 things to do

_____

_____

_____

_____

_____

Daily Mindset Habits   Date _____

___ Wake Up Early

___ Morning Gratitude

___ Write Down Goals in Detail

___ Exercise (Walk, Run, Jump Etc..)

___ Read Something Positive

___ Pray / Meditate

Goals for the Month:

_____

_____

_____

_____

_____

_____

_____

_____

What Went Well (write down everything, no victory too small)

_____

_____

_____

_____

_____

_____

_____

Tomorrow's top 3 things to do

_____

_____

_____

_____

_____

About the Publisher

BookFamous is dedicated to helping busy Entrepreneurs, Speakers, Coaches and Consultants become published authors so that they can Increase their Influence, Leverage their Message and Expand their Brand. We leverage the trust, credibility and opportunities a book can create for you. We also understand that it can be confusing, scary and time consuming to create one. That's why we are here. To make it simple, fun and stress-free. Our ultimate goal is to create a seamless and pleasant client experience and produce a World Class Product you can be proud of. We look forward helping you share and preserve your story in your own book soon!

Free Publishing Master Class go to www.BookFamous.com

BF

BOOK FAMOUS

Manhattan Beach, Ca

888-266-5387

Marcos@BookFamous.com

www.ingramcontent.com/pod-product-compliance
Lightning Source LLC
Chambersburg PA
CBHW021935190326
41519CB00009B/1027